S

Teacher's resource

150

YEAR
5

Literacy Hour
Lessons

Contents	Page
How to use this book	3
Summary of objectives	5
Autumn term lesson plans	8
Spring term lesson plans	28
Summer term lesson plans	48
Copymasters	68
Homework copymasters	128

Acknowledgements

The author and publisher would like to thank the following for permission to reproduce material in this book: 'Right' by David Williams (from 'Mr Jones Versus Angela' ed. John Foster) reproduced by permission of Oxford University Press. 'The Hodgeheg' by Dick King-Smith reproduced by permission of A.P Watt. 'Hooray for Howard' by Colin West reproduced by permission of HarperCollins. Cover blurb from 'Boy' by Roald Dahl (Puffin, 1986). Copyright © Penguin Books Ltd., 1986. Reproduced by permission of Penguin UK. Cover blurb from 'The Goalkeeper's Revenge' by Bill Naughton (Puffin, 1968). Copyright © Penguin Books Ltd., 1968. Reproduced by permission of Penguin UK Cover blurb from 'The Jungle Books' by Rudyard Kipling (Penguin Classics, 1989). Copyright © Penguin Books Ltd., 1989. Reproduced by permission of Penguin UK. Cover blurb from 'War Boy' by Michael Foreman (Puffin, 1991) Copyright © Penguin Books Ltd., 1991. Reproduced by permission of Penguin UK. Cover blurb from 'The Suitcase Kid' by Jacqueline Wilson reproduced by permission of Yearling Books. Cover blurb from 'Friend or Foe' © 1977 Michael Morpurgo. First published by Mammoth in 1989, an imprint of Egmont Books Limited and used with permission. 'Rolling Down a Hill' by Colin West (from 'The Upside Down Frown') reproduced by permission of Wayland Publishers Ltd. 'Caterpillars' by Leigh Woods (first published in 'Hands on Poetry. Using Poetry in the Classroom' edited by Sue Ellis with Myra Barrs. London: Centre for Language in Primary Education. 1995. Reproduced by permission of the Centre for Language in Primary Education. 'Superstink' by Robert Froman (from the 'Kingfisher Book of Children's Poetry'). 'Hickory Dickory Dock', 'Old Mother Hubbard', (Humpty Dumpty' and Fried Fresh Fish' by Michael Rosen (from 'Walking on the Bridge of My Nose'). 'Rebecca' and 'Jack and his Pony, Tom' by Hilaire Belloc reproduced by permission of the Peters Fraser and Dunlop Group. 'Spells' and 'The Intruder' © James Reeves from 'Complete Poems for Children' published by Heinemann. Reprinted by permission of the James Reeves Estate. 'Nettles' by Vernon Scannell reproduced by permission of the author. 'The Weather' by Gavin Ewart (from 'Footprints on the Page' published by Evans Publishing Group).'Benny McEever' by Gareth Owen (from 'A Stack of Story Poems' ed. Tony Bradman) reproduced by permission of the author. 'Keeping Cool' (from 'Deserts') by Jenny Wood reproduced by permission of Two-Can Publishing.

The following titles are in the public domain but the publisher acknowledges the use of extracts from the following material: 'White Fang' by Jack London. 'The Way Through the Woods' by Rudyard Kipling. 'Three Fishers Went Sailing' by Charles Kingsley.

Every effort has been made to trace and acknowledge ownership of copyright material but if any have been inadvertently overlooked, the publisher will be pleased to make the necessary alterations at the first opportunity.

First published 2001
exclusively for WHSmith by

Hodder & Stoughton Educational,
a division of Hodder Headline Ltd.
338 Euston Road
London NW1 3BH

Text and illustrations ©Hodder & Stoughton Educational 2001

A CIP record for this book is available from the British Library.

Author: Kay Hiatt
Series editor: Gill Matthews

ISBN 0340 79000 8

Impression number   10 9 8 7 6 5
Year   2006 2005

Typeset by Fakenham Photosetting
Printed and bound in Spain by Graphycems

Each term is divided into ten weekly themes, organised as follows:

• Objectives for the week

These are taken from the National Literacy Strategy Framework for Teaching and form the basis of medium term planning for text, word and sentence level work.

• Resources

A list of the materials that are needed to teach the theme. Some themes are generic and a range of texts could be used while others are written around suggested texts.

Where necessary, preparation that can be carried out in advance is highlighted.

• Assessment

This is an outline of broad assessment objectives, recognising that many teachers already have detailed recording and assessment procedures in place in their schools.

• Lesson outlines

Each lesson is divided into the following sections:

Whole class

This section contains suggestions for whole class shared reading or writing activities. The final outcome of most themes is a completed piece of written work. The whole class teaching aims to guide children through the objectives in order to achieve this.

Group and independent work

This section contains ideas for group work, whether guided by you or another adult, or independent work. The suggested activity may be the task that you focus on with a group. How these activities are used will depend on your particular organisation.

Differentiation

Most lessons are accompanied by differentiated activities for high and low attainers and suggestions for where it would be suitable for children to work in mixed ability pairs.

Whole class

The final section of each lesson gives ideas for a plenary session, including:

- activities which revisit key learning objectives;
- feedback from children, either individuals, pairs or in some cases the whole class, on the work they have been doing;

- feedback from children on a partner's work;
- preparation for the next day's lesson;
- class evaluation of a lesson or a theme of work.

• Photocopiable masters (copymasters)

Most themes are accompanied by photocopiable masters for use in whole class and group time. These are not work sheets to practise taught skills, but are closely linked to the content of the lesson. Many can be used as frames for collecting discussed ideas or for shared writing in whole class sessions, as well as by the children in group or independent work.

• Homework

Each theme is accompanied by a photocopiable homework sheet which explains to parents or guardians what the children have been doing in literacy work for that particular week. This is followed by a task that can be carried out by the child.

Throughout the themes the development of reading and writing skills are linked closely. Themes or blocks of themes start with an emphasis on the teaching of reading through shared reading, use the reading as a stimulus or model for shared writing and suggest ideas for children's writing based on the shared work that has been carried out.

Shared reading

The different reading organisations covered include:
- teacher reading to the children;
- children reading with the teacher;
- class reading without the teacher joining in;
- a group reading to the rest of the class;
- individual children reading to the class.

Shared writing

This book suggests activities whereby teachers model writing, provide a scaffold to support children in their writing and teach writing over a sequence of lessons. Children's writing should be used in shared sessions as a means of encouraging the early stages of drafting and improving writing.

Word level work

In order to ensure the appropriate emphasis and

focus it is often better to introduce word level work separately from text level work. Teachers will lead children in using their word level skills within shared reading and writing.

• Phonics

Phonic work should be used to support reading and children should be encouraged to see links between phonic activities, and shared and guided reading activities. Phonic work should also be incorporated into shared writing activities. Children can be encouraged to use word lists generated in phonic work to help with spellings. Many children find a class-made 'long vowel' dictionary a useful writing support.

• Word recognition, graphic knowledge and spelling

Word walls, lists and cards are ways of displaying and drawing children's attention to words that need to become part of their sight vocabulary. Recognition and practice of these words can be incorporated into shared and guided work.

• Handwriting

Most schools have adopted a particular handwriting scheme and many teachers have taken the practising of handwriting out of the Literacy Hour. However, modelled and shared writing provide good opportunities to demonstrate handwriting.

Teaching and learning strategies

A range of teaching techniques are suggested to make lessons interactive and ensure the involvement of all children. These include:

- Use of the 'time out' strategy during whole class sessions where pairs or small groups of children are given short periods of time to discuss a question, think of an appropriate word or compose a sentence.
- Pairing children during group work to encourage discussion and develop collaborative skills.
- Feedback from the class when sitting in a circle.
- Use of small whiteboards. These can be purchased from suppliers or made by laminating card and used with appropriate pens.
- Many teachers now make use of large whiteboards for shared writing and related activities. Large sheets of sugar paper may be more appropriate for some activities as they can be:
  - displayed as a model for writing;

- used as part of a 'work in progress' display;
- referred to as a memory jogger;
- re-read as a familiar text, which can be particularly useful for low attaining children.

Speaking and listening

A range of suggestions for the inclusion of speaking and listening are included such as:

- organising a range of audiences for reading and for the sharing of written work;
- encouraging children to listen to each other in discussion about aspects of texts;
- asking children to respond to a range of questions, to give opinions and share ideas;
- making use of drama techniques such as 'hotseating', where some children are encouraged to take on a role and others to ask questions, during whole class work.

ICT

The amount of use made of ICT depends on many factors such as the hardware available and teachers' confidence in using it. A range of suggestions for its use are offered.

Word processing
The majority of writing activities that are carried out with paper and pencil can be fulfilled using a word processing package. Children's lack of word processing skills often makes tasks such as producing a final copy of a piece of written work laborious and time consuming. However, opportunities for word processing can be organised through tasks such as creating captions, labels, book titles and headings.

The Internet
The Internet may be used to find information relating to fiction and non-fiction work.

E-mail
There are a growing number of local, national and international projects making use of the school e-mail address to develop links with other groups and share information and ideas.

Word and sentence level activities
There are a growing number of programs available to support spelling development and the learning of certain grammatical structures.

Autumn term

	Theme	Objectives: children will be taught to:
1	Non-fiction	Identify the features of recounted texts such as sports reports, diaries, police reports. Write recounts based on subject, topic or personal experience for a) a close friend and b) an unknown reader. Understand the basic conventions of standard English. Understand the difference between direct and reported speech.
2	Playscripts	Understand dramatic conventions including: • the conventions of scripting • how character can be communicated in words and gesture • how tension can be filled up through paces, silences and delivery. Write their own playscript, applying conventions learnt through reading. Annotate a section of playscript as a preparation for performance, taking into account pace, movement, gesture and the delivery of lines and the needs of the audience. Evaluate the script and the perfomance for their dramatic interest and impact. Discuss, proof-read and edit their own writing.
3	Note-taking	Discuss the purpose of note taking and how this influences the purpose of notes made. Make notes for different purposes and build on these notes in their own writing or speaking. Make simple abbreviations in note taking.
4	Story openings	Analyse the features of a good opening and compare a number of story openings. Experiment with alternative ways of opening a story, e.g. description, action, dialogue. Compare the structure of different stories: pace, build-up, sequence, complication and resolution. Map out texts showing development and structure. Discuss, proof-read and edit their own writing. Understand the need for punctuation as an aid to the reader. Understand how to set out dialogue.
5	Fiction characters in stories	Investigate how characters are presented, referring to the text: • through dialogue, action and description and how the reader responds to them • through examining their relationships with other characters. Develop an active attitude towards reading. Write new scenes or characters into the story in the manner of the writer. Set out dialogue.
6	Book reviews	Consider how texts can be rooted in the writer's experience. Evaluate a book by referring to details and examples in the text. Discuss the enduring appeal of established authors. Record their ideas, reflections and predictions about a book.
7	Non-fiction	Read and evaluate a range of instructional texts in terms of their purpose, organisation, layout, clarity and usefulness. Write instructional texts and test them out. Revise and extend work on verbs, focusing on tense, form and person. Identify the imperative form in instructional writing.
8	Word play and the writing of metaphors	Investigate and collect different examples of word play, relating form to meaning. Write metaphors from original ideas or similes.
9	Comparing two different poets	Read a number of poems by significant poets and identify what is distinctive about the style or content of their poems. Analyse and compare poetic style, use of form and themes of significant poets. Respond to shades of meaning. Explain and justify personal tastes. Consider the impact of full rhymes, half rhymes, internal rhymes and other sound patterns. Convey feelings, reflections or moods in a poem through the careful selection of words and phrases. Explain the differences between synonyms. Collect, classify and order sets of words to identify shades of meaning.
10	Word order	Investigate word order by examining how far the order of words in sentences can be changed: • which words are essential to meaning? • which can be removed without damaging the basic meaning? • which words or groups of words can be moved into a different order? Discuss, proof-read and edit their own writing, creating more complex sentences. Adapt writing for different readers and purposes, e.g. younger audiences. Understand the need for punctuation as an aid to the reader, e.g. commas to mark grammatical boundaries; a colon to signal a list.

Summary of objectives

Spring term

	Theme	Objectives: children will be taught to:
1	Poems	Read a range of narrative poems. Perform poems in a variety of ways. Understand terms which describe different sorts of poems. Understand the difference between literal and figurative language. Use the structure of poems read to write extensions based on these.
2	Oral storytelling	Explore similarities and differences between oral and written storytelling. Make notes of story outline as a preparation for oral storytelling.
3	Explanations	Read a range of explanatory texts, investigating and noting features of impersonal style. Plan, compose, edit and refine short non-chronological reports and explanatory texts using reading as a source, focusing on clarity, conciseness and impersonal style. Evaluate their own work. Explore ambiguities that arise from sentence contractions, e.g. through signs and headlines.
4	Punctuation	Use punctuation effectively to signpost meaning in longer and more complex sentences. Construct sentences in different ways, while maintaining meaning, through: • combining two or more sentences • re-ordering them • deleting or substituting words • writing them in more telegraphic ways. Secure the use of the comma in embedding clauses within sentences.
5	Fiction, film and print	Investigate different versions of the same story in print or on film, identifying similarities and differences. Recognise how stories change over time and differences of culture and place that are expresses in stories..
6	Difference between author and narrator	Distinguish between the author and the narrator, investigating narrative viewpoint and the treatment of different characters. Investigate the features of different fiction genres, discussing the appeal of popular fiction.
7	Myths, legends and fables	Identify and classify the features of myths, legends and fables. Write their own versions of myths, legends and fables, using structures and themes identified in reading. Review and edit their writing to produce a final form, matched to the needs of an identified reader. Understand how writing can be adapted to different audiences and purposes. Ensure that, in using pronouns, it is clear to what or to whom they refer.
8	Non-chronological reports	Prepare for reading by identifying what they know already and what they need to find out. Locate information confidently and efficiently through: • using contents, indexes, sections and headings; • skimming to gain overall sense of the text; • scanning to locate specific information; • reading closely to aid understanding; • text-marking; • using CD and other sources, where available. Plan, compose, edit and refine short non-chronological reports, using reading as a source, focusing on clarity, conciseness and impersonal style.
9	Information sources	Understand how authors record and acknowledge their sources. Evaluate texts critically by comparing how different sources treat the same information. Discuss what is meant by 'in your own words' and when it is appropriate to copy, quote and adapt. Record and acknowledge sources in their own writing.
10	Poetry anthologies	Compile a class anthology of favourite poems with commentaries which illuminate their choices. Use the structure of poems to write extensions based on these.

Summer term

	Theme	Objectives: children will be taught to:
1	Writing from different cultures	Investigate a range of texts from different cultures, considering patterns of relationships, social customs, attitudes and beliefs. Identify these features by reference to the text. Consider and evaluate these features in relation to their own experience. Write discursively about a novel or story, e.g. to describe, explain or comment on it.
2	Points of view	Identify the point of view from which a story is told and how this affects the reader's response. Change the point of view, e.g. describe a situation or incident from another character's point of view or from a different perspective. Write from another character's point of view, e.g. retell an incident in letter form. Write in the style of the author.
3	Poetry	Read, rehearse and modify performance of poetry. Select poetry, justify their choices, eg. in compiling their class anthology. Use performance poems as models to write and produce poetry in polished forms, through revising, redrafting and presentation. Use a range of dictionaries and understand their purposes, e.g. idioms.
4	Letters	Read and evaluate letters, e.g. from newspapers or magazines, which are intended to inform, protest, complain or persuade. Consider: • how they are set out; • how language is used (e.g. to gain attention or respect, to manipulate); Draft and write individual, group or class letters for real purposes, e.g. putting forward a point of view, commenting, protesting. Edit and present a letter in a finished state.
5	Advertisements	Read and evaluate adverts or fliers. Consider: • the deliberate use of ambiguity, half-truth and bias; • how opinion can be disguised to look like fact. Select a range of texts and evaluate for their persuasiveness. Investigate, from reading, the use of persuasive devices, e.g. words and phrases, rhetorical questions, deliberate ambiguities. Write examples of these.
6	Persuasion	Select a range of texts in print or other media and evaluate them for their persuasiveness. Construct an argument in note form or full to persuade others of a point of view, present it to the class or group and evaluate its effectiveness.
7	Using dictionaries	Use a range of dictionaries and understand their purposes. Use dictionaries efficiently to explore spellings, meanings or derivations. Compile their own class or group dictionary, using personally written definitions of, for example, slang or technical terms.
8	Poetry	Change the point of view. Read, rehearse and modify performance poetry. Write from another character's point of view.
9	'Classics'	Explore the challenge and appeal of older literature through: listening to older literature being read aloud; • reading accessible stories, poems and extracts; • reading extracts from classics serials shown on television; • discussing differences in the language used. Record predictions, questions and reflection while reading. Write in the style of the author.
10	Grammar	Secure the basic conventions of standard English sentence construction and punctuation. Investigate clauses through: • identifying the main clause in a long sentence; • investigating sentences which have more than one clause; • understanding how clauses are connected, e.g. by combining three short sentences into one.

Theme 1) Non-fiction

Objectives

Text level
- 21 to identify the features of recounted texts such as sports reports, diaries, police reports
- 24 to write recounts based on subject, topic or personal experience for (a) a close friend and (b) an unknown reader

Sentence level
- to understand the basic conventions of standard English
- to understand the difference between direct and reported speech

Resources
Samples of recounts; sports reports; crime reports taken from newspapers; information books from other curriculum areas, especially history; pupils' recounts from previous year groups as part of cross-curricular work; biographies; extracts from diaries; school newspaper recounts of team games or visits etc.
Copymaster 1 – A visit to London.
Copymaster 2 – A sports report.
Homework 1.

Assessment
At the end of this theme is the pupil able to:
- identify the features of recounted texts;
- use these features in their own writing for: (a) a close friend and (b) an unknown audience;
- be aware of the importance of standard English in texts to an unknown audience;
- understand the difference between direct and reported speech?

Lesson 1

Whole class

Explain to the class that in this unit they will be learning about the features of recounts. This will enable them to write recounts themselves for a friend and for someone they do not know. They will also be learning about the importance of standard English when writing to someone they have never met, as well as the differences between direct and reported speech.
Using an OHT or a large version of the recount on Copymaster 1, read it aloud to the pupils.
Explain that the purpose of a recount is to retell events. Recounts should offer information on When, Where, What, Who, and Why. Write these words on separate cards. These are the **5 'W'** cards. Fix them on the board then ask pupils to read a card, *e.g. What*, and by referring to the recount to explain what happened. Do the same for *Who* and get a pupil to state who is mentioned in the recount. Continue with the other **'W'** cards. Then give pupils 2 minutes to notice other features as follows: scene setting introduction; series of events in time order; time connectives: when, then, next, before, meanwhile, after that, during, later, finally; written (mainly) in the past tense; a closing statement

Explain that the recount is written in standard English so that anyone can understand it.

Group and independent work
Ask the class to create their own recounted text incorporating the **5 'W's** and using the identified language features.
They can either choose to write about a school trip they can remember well, or a recount of a visit they have recently been on. Say that they are writing this for an unknown audience, *e.g. for a parent/governor/Ofsted inspector to read*, so it must be in standard English.
When they have finished, they must check that their recount has incorporated the **5 'W's**.

Differentiation
Low Attainers – Can be given a simple writing frame with the time connectives already written in.
High Attainers – Can be asked to produce a class poster based on your class input on the typical structure of a recount – **5 'W's** + other features.

Whole class
Ask 4 pupils to read out their recounts. The class will check as they go along that these contain the information needed in a recount from the **5 'W'** cards and from the poster designed by the high attaining group.

Lesson 2

Whole class

Use an OHP or an enlarged text of a sports report – Copymaster 2. Read it, checking the **5 'W's** as you go. Ask children what the differences are between this and the 'Visit to London' recount. Show them the other text if they cannot remember. Say that it was written for a local newspaper, so the audience is unknown: standard English is essential.

Group and independent work
Give each group examples of sports reports and ask them in pairs to make a table in their books.
On the left-hand side write the type of text it is and a headline; on the right hand side, list the text features as they appear. Expect them to refer to the poster produced in the previous lesson.

Differentiation
Low Attainers – Can be given a cut up version of a sports report. Ask them to reconstruct it in the correct order, then check it against the poster of recount features.
High Attainers – Read a present tense version of the recount, and compare it to the original version. Is it better, or not?

Whole class
Ask the high attaining group to feed back, reflecting upon what they have learned.
Ensure that children understand that sports reports are recounts.

Lesson 3

Whole class

Explain that you are going to demonstrate how to write a crime report. Use the one below, if you wish. As you write, think aloud for the children, offering them a running commentary of how you are keeping to the requirements of the text type. Remember to mention that you are writing in standard English.

Lay out this text as a newspaper report: *Up to her tricks again! Goldilocks' mother was said to be very depressed after the news of her daughter's trespass into the Three Bears' cottage yesterday. She was seen at the window in tears when local reporters gathered around to watch the Forest Police arrive. The local constable looked very concerned when he left her bungalow. He told the waiting reporters: 'Leave this woman alone. She needs some peace and quiet, especially after the row with Mr Bear yesterday.' Goldilocks has not been seen since yesterday. It is rumoured that she is staying with her neighbours, the Hoods.*

Group and independent work

Ask pupils in pairs to write a crime report on either of the following scenarios:

1. *Harp leads to Jack's Capture* (crime report about Jack's theft of the harp)
2. *Concussion for Jack and Jill* (crime report about their accident with the pail)

They must follow the structure and contain the previously identified typical features of recounts.

Differentiation

Low Attainers – Can be given a simple frame to get them started.

High Attainers – Can build into their recounts a piece of dialogue in which Jack defends himself or a witness is reported as saying that Jill was to blame.

Whole class

Ask a high attainment group to read out their crime reports, stopping at the dialogue and asking the class to guess what the person actually said.

Lesson 4

Whole class

Using a dialogue extract written yesterday as part of the crime reports, get the pupils who wrote it to say it out loud.

Then write down the whole sentence, including the spoken words, *e.g Jack shouted: 'It wasn't me who stole the harp!'* Write DIRECT SPEECH above the sentence.

Now show them how to change this into REPORTED SPEECH: *Jack shouted that it was not him who had stolen the harp.*

Ask for another pair's contribution and follow the same procedure.

Now ask for volunteers to read out their direct speech and give the class 1 minute each to write it down as reported speech.

Group and independent activities

Referring to a selection of fiction books, ask pupils to collect three examples of direct speech and three examples of reported speech and write them in their books under the correct headings.

Differentiation

Low Attainers – Find 2 examples each of direct and indirect speech and write them on a sheet with the prepared headings and one example of each already written as a model.

High Attainers – Prepare a short oral argument where a brother/sister accuses a friend of borrowing their latest CD without permission. Then they must write together a reported version of the quarrel using no direct speech.

Whole class

Ask the class to give a definition of direct speech, reported speech and the need for writing to unknown audiences in standard English.

Lesson 5

Whole class

Quickly show both recounts from Copymasters 1 and 2. Remind them that these were all written for an unknown audience.

Now tell them that you will write the sports report for a friend this time, in a much more informal way, on a postcard. Use this model, if you wish:

Dear Tom
Well we was really thrashed last Saturday! The field was like a mudbath, and I slipped and fell over and twisted me knee. Will be glad to see you'se back in the team.
Regards Al

Ask them what differences they notice (non-standard English; implicit that your friend will understand what you are writing). Is it still a recount?

Group and independent work

Individually, ask pupils to select a recount from another curricular area, *e.g. history*, and to re-write it as a postcard to a friend. They can use non-standard English if they wish.

Differentiation

Low Attainers – Can read a recount which has had the direct speech deleted, and add this in. Say they will be reading their sentences out in the plenary session and the rest of the class will have to guess what the recount was about.

High Attainers – Can use the London visit text and re-write it as a newspaper report, including dialogue.

Whole class

Ask the low attaining group to read out their sentences. The class must guess what the recount was about. Reflect on learning. Ensure that children understand the purpose and structure of recounts and that sports, crime and newspaper reports are recounts.

Theme 2) Playscripts

Objectives

Text level
- 5 to understand dramatic conventions including:
  - the conventions of scripting
  - how character can be communicated in words and gesture
  - how tension can be filled up through pace, silences and delivery
- to write own playscript, applying conventions applied from reading
- to annotate a section of playscript as a preparation for performance, taking into account pace, movement, gesture and delivery of lines and the needs of audience
- to evaluate the script and the performance for their dramatic interest and impact

Sentence level
- 3   to discuss, proof-read and edit their own writing.

Resources
Copymaster 3 – Pages 14 and 15 of the playscript (minus illustration) of 'Right' by David Williams from *Mr Jones Versus Angela*.
Copymaster 4 – Pages 16–19 of the same playscript
Copy of *James and the Giant Peach*.
Homework 2.

Assessment
At the end of this theme is the pupil able to:
- write his/her own playscript using the features of playscripts, and produce a well presented, published version for a class Big Book;
- annotate a playscript, giving advice on words, gesture, movement and pace?

Lesson 1

Whole class

Explain to the class that the aims of this theme are to learn about plays: how they work, how to prepare a playscript for performance, and how to write one themselves.

Sit the pupils in a circle.

Put up on the OHT an enlarged Copymaster 3.

Ask pupils to read it silently and tell you about the layout (characters' names on left hand side, no speech marks, new lines for each character), and the characters of Les and Tim.

Ask them how the author wants an audience to feel when watching this play.

Using the whiteboard, write the two headings **Clues to how the character is feeling: movement/gesture, Clues to how a character is feeling: tone of voice/pace of delivery** then ask pupils to suggest words to describe the contrasting characters (they can do this in pairs on their small whiteboards). Then add their suggestions to the table.

Choose two pupils to be Les and Tim and get them to stand in the circle.

Ask them to act out the scene from the OHT model. The rest of the class watches then makes up to 5 positive comments followed by 2 suggestions for improvement – they show 'how to' by moving into the circle and demonstrating to the 'actors' how to do it.

Group work
Give out sections of the copymasters to various groups of three pupils. Ask them to read them. After they have done this ask them to add in to the table any other words which offer clues as to how each character is feeling as the script unfolds.

Differentiation
The children can work in mixed ability groups for this work.

Whole class
Return to the circle and share pupils' notes; ask one or two pupils to move into the circle and demonstrate what they mean. Include pupils who have thought about pace of delivery, as this is a harder concept.

Lesson 2

Whole Class

Tell pupils that you want them to prepare their section of the script for performance, paying careful attention to their notes from yesterday

Demonstrate how to do this using the model below, talking through what you are doing e.g. the need for stage directions at the beginning and adding in 'How to' suggestions in note format along the side of the text:

Stage Directions	
(Tim stands in the playground – head down, shoulders drooped, hands in pockets.	
He starts walking across the playground, slowly, still looking down.	
Les rushes on to the playground, and catches up with Tim)	
Les Hey, you!	*Jabs finger into back, yelling*
Tim Who? Me?	*Half turns, startled, surprised*
Les You I'm talking to. You	*'You' loud, sneering*

Group Work
Pupils complete the task.

Whole Class: sitting in a circle
Choose one group to first read out their notes on

performance and then act it out, the whole class evaluating how well they did it, awarding points out of 5 for words, gesture, movement and pace

Lesson 3

Whole Class

Put up an extract of Roald Dahl's James and the Giant Peach – Chap 15, first page up to 'Both women swung around to have a look.'
Model what you have to do to change this extract into a playscript, up to the sentence 'We shall make a fortune today. Just look at all those people!'
Teacher Demonstration
• Change the word 'chapter' to 'Act'
• Add stage directions at the beginning,
• Write the names of the characters down the left-hand side
• Write what they say alongside, no speech marks required
• Add in more stage directions if needed (if characters need to move to a different position on stage)

Then ask for the pupils' contributions to finish off the extract.

Group and independent work, including differentiation 1

Give each pupil extracts from James and the Giant Peach, and ask them to turn it into a playscript. Suggested pages as follows:
Low Attainers – Opening 12 lines of Chap 6 up to 'let alone a peach'.
High Attainers – Chap 3 (stage directions essential)
Middle Groups : end of Chap 2, beginning 'Great tears began oozing out of James' eyes.' to the end of the chapter.
Encourage discussion between pupils.

Whole Class

Take contributions from each group on how easy/difficult they found this task.

Lesson 4 (extended writing session)

Whole Class – Independent Work

In pairs, all of the class will continue to change their story extracts into a playscript.
Using post-it notes, they should write quick notes on speech and gesture, as modelled in lesson 2.
Teacher joins each group 'at the point of writing' and offers constructive criticism on the work in process.

She refers to the bullet point list from lesson 3 which is printed on a laminated sheet on each table; a larger version is on the wall.
Collect this work in and return it the following day marked for :
• Correct lay out of playscript.
• Quality of advice on post-its.

Lesson 5

Group Work (Use the hall or push back the desks)

Ask pupils to group themselves into sets with correct no. of characters and one 'director' per set.
Prepare for performance, the director selecting from the

post-it notes those he/she thinks are most useful and giving advice on words, gesture, movement and pace.

Evaluation

One pupil in each group has a blank template, which they fill, in following discussion with their group.
Starters are given which help to speed up the process.
Points are awarded out of 5 for each aspect of delivery.

Theme 3) Note-taking

Objectives

Text level
• 23 to discuss the purpose of note-taking and how this influences the purpose of notes made
• 26 to make notes for different purposes and to build on these notes in their own writing or speaking
• 27 to make simple abbreviations in note taking

Resources
A selection of books related to another curriculum areas including ICT texts; video material; adult English dictionaries.
Copymaster 5. Homework 3.

Assessment
At the end of this theme is the pupil able to:
• discuss the purposes of note-taking and different ways of doing it linked to the end product;
• make notes for different purposes and use them for the purposes of speaking and writing;
• use simple abbreviations as an aspect of note-taking?

Lesson 1

Whole class

Use 30 minutes to introduce note-taking. Explain to the class that note-taking is important for taking out the *important bits you need* for some research e.g. in science. Gather a selection of texts which are all about the same thing, *e.g. Life Processes and Living Things if you are studying this in science.*
Say that you are going to show them how to make notes for a leaflet on slugs and snails under the headings: feeding, movement, growth, reproduction, habitat.
Enlarge one of these texts or use as an OHT and read it aloud. Run through each heading in turn, making notes as you go. Leave out words like *it, the, and* – you want as few words as possible. Write each heading on the whiteboard. Demonstrate how to write your notes under each heading, e.g. SLUGS Feeding → at night → lettuce, tomatoes, strawberries.
When you have made as many notes as are useful from the text, ask the class to count the number of words in your notes, then tell them how many words the whole text contained. Tell them that note-taking is not copying out whole sentences – you just extract the most important bits you need.

Group and independent work
Hand out photocopies of other texts on the same subject.
Say that you want no more than 30 words taken as notes from the text.
Get the pupils to write notes on post-its and stick them under relevant headings.

Differentiation
Mixed Ability Groups – All work on the same task, low attainers reading more accessible texts.

Whole class
Start off this session by asking what pupils learnt about note-taking.
Read aloud a selection of their notes and ask the class to agree whether these are useful and brief.

Lesson 2

Whole Class

Start off this session by asking them what they learnt about note-taking.
Put up a set of key facts about Roald Dahl: successful writer, child & adult books, awards – Matilda, BFG, unhappy – boarding school, Royal Air Force – fighter pilot, inventor –life-saving valves, script – James Bond film 'You Only Live Twice'.
Demonstrate how to write a 'Newsshot'- an interesting snapshot of important things a person did in their lives (source – books on writers/ inventors /explorers/ scientists). Import a picture or photograph to go with your newsshot. Use the model below, thinking aloud for pupils about the required features of a 'newsshot'.
Roald Dahl (1918-1990) was one of the century's most important writers for both children and adults. After an unhappy start at boarding school, he went on to lead a very exciting life – as a fighter pilot, a spy and a life-saving inventor as well as a screen-writer and best selling author. Several of his books won awards – Matilda and the BFG.
What you talk about as you write:
First Sentence
• subject of snapshot in bold font
• dates of life span in brackets
• finish this sentence with information on the most famous thing he did
Second Sentence
Start with a phrase beginning with 'after' giving one fact about early life
• Continue with: 'he went on to lead a .... life'
• Add in a dash then one, two or three key facts
• Join to the rest of the sentence with 'as well as' followed by one or two facts
Third Sentence
• Add one more sentence to round off the newsshot.

Group and independent work
Give out different copies of pages of information on an explorer/inventor/scientist/engineer and ask them to prepare a 'newsshot'

Differentiation
In pairs, *attainers* can be given half of the notes from a text and finish remaining notes using close exercises
High Attainers – Can produce notes on a famous person from encyclopaedias

Whole Class
Ask the low achieving group to read out their notes and test if the class can re-work them into sentence form for a 'Newsshot'

Lesson 3

Whole class

Model how to make different sorts of notes: cartoon-type drawings, diagrams, charts, flow charts.
Explain that it is better to use a flow chart for notes when you are trying to describe a process of some kind.
Demonstrate how the notes in the flow chart can be transformed into text.

Group and independent work

Give out extracts of texts from science or geography which describe a process, *e.g. making of glass, paper or steel; the water cycle.*
Ask pupils to make notes and put them in a flow chart and then ask another pair to make sense of this.

Differentiation

Low Attainers – Can use Copymaster 5 – put a flow chart in the right order and then explain the process to a friend.
High Attainers – Can produce a flow chart on an OHT or large sheet of paper.

Whole class

Ask the high attaining group to explain the meaning of their flow charts.

Lesson 4

Whole class

Watch a short video together linked to another curriculum area.
Write key headings on the board.
Re-play the video and ask the class to take notes under these headings; they can choose which form the notes will take.
Their notes will be used to prepare a quiz for the class.

Group and independent work

Using their notes, each pair of pupils should prepare 10 questions to ask the class.

Differentiation

Low Attainers – Can be given a set of questions with key words missing, and work them out from their notes.
High Attainers – Can prepare a poster to inform parents of the importance of note-taking, and give examples of the forms they have used.

Whole class

Divide the class in half and run the quiz, using the questions the children have prepared.

Lesson 5

Whole class

Write up a selection of abbreviations and ask why abbreviating words might be useful for someone making notes (brevity/speed).
Write up a selection of abbreviations and see if pupils can 'read' them. Find these at the front of most adult dictionaries.
Now investigate some e-mail acronyms, again used for speed and brevity, *e.g. AFAIR as far as I remember; BFN bye for now; ASAP as soon a possible; ROTFL rolling on the floor laughing; CU see you; IMO in my opinion; WHAVGT = was having a very good time.*
Write these in a sentence: *AFAIR we all saw him at the party. He WHAVGT; the pretty girl he was with said BFN and xxx him three times!*

Group and independent work

Ask the groups to conduct some investigations into:
- shorthand forms by reading newspaper small ads section;
- opening letter pages in a dictionary.

Differentiation

Low Attainers – Write a list of abbreviations from small ads and say what they mean.
High Attainers – Can compose a message on a computer, incorporating some acronyms, and send it to a friend or parent.

Whole class

Ask the class to think about the objectives for this theme; you scribe their suggestions then show them the actual ones, as above. Congratulate them on being very close to the originals!

Theme 4) Story openings

Objectives

Text level

- 1 to analyse the features of a good opening and compare a number of story openings
- 2 to compare the structure of different stories: pace, build-up, sequence, complication and resolution
- 11 to experiment with alternative ways of opening a story, e.g. description, action, dialogue
- 14 to map out texts showing development and structure

Sentence level

- 3 to discuss, proof-read and edit their own writing
- 6/7 to understand the need for punctuation as an aid to the reader and how to set out dialogue

Resources

Copymaster 6: different openings + caption cards.
Copymaster 7: a flow chart analysis of The Hodgeheg.
Homework 4.

Assessment

At the end of this theme is the pupil able to:

- identify the different ways in which stories begin and incorporate these features in his/her own writing;
- know about story structure and analyse stories and reflect upon this as a basis for planning his/her own stories?

Lesson 1

Whole class

Read out the selected openings from different stories. Use your voice expressively to catch pupils' interest; pause after each opening, then move on to the next one. Explain that writers put a lot of time, effort and thought into how they can best open their story. They want you to read on – and buy their book!

Put up the three caption cards from the bottom of Copymaster 6 and ask them to match each opening to the card; ask how each writer catches the interest of the reader, and which opening they like best – and why. Explain that what they have done are the objectives for this lesson: comparing story openings and noticing how each writer focuses on a different aspect of story structure.

Group and independent work

Place a selection of books on each table with a set of the three caption cards and some blank cards. Ask pupils in pairs to read the opening page(s) and decide under which caption to place the book. If it does not fit the style of opening, write another caption on a blank card.

Differentiation

Low Attainers – Select openings from books which are within their reading ability and complete the same activity.
High Attainers – Can be asked to analyse *The Hodgeheg* opening in more depth, *e.g. does the dialogue convey any information about the characters?*

Whole class

Ask a pair from each table to read out an opening and then the class decides which caption card is the best fit.

Lesson 2

Whole class

Ask the class what they learned yesterday about story openings.

Explain that you are now going to write an opening of a story using one of the approaches used from yesterday's OHT.

Use the dialogue example from *The Hodgeheg* as this will support understanding of the importance of punctuation as an aid to the reader.

Think aloud as you speak, stating the punctuation rules for dialogue as you go along. Comment that the dialogue introduces a problem of some kind (the girl crying) which the story will develop.

Group and independent work

Give each group a different scenario, *e.g. first sight of an alien, a hidden valley, a house on fire, a thief in a* supermarket, a lost child and ask each pupil to write independently a piece of dialogue between two characters, which must be correctly punctuated. They are to use *The Hodgeheg* model as you did.

Differentiation

Low Attainers – Could be given a piece of dialogue already started.
High Attainers – Must incorporate some verbs other than 'said' in their piece of dialogue – verbs which offer a clue to the characters' feelings.
You may need to demonstrate this first as part of a guided writing session for this group.

Whole class

Ask pupils to give you a list of bullet point rules for punctuating dialogue and write this as a poster.

Lesson 3

Whole class

Start off the lesson by referring to yesterday's writing when pupils used a piece of dialogue to get the story moving.

Now return to *The Hodgeheg* and reveal how the author structured this story by using Copymaster 7.

Underline the problem in green, conflicts as the plot develops in orange, red for the climax and blue for the resolution.

As you read this chart, draw a graph to illustrate the ups and downs of the story, clearly linked to pace. Use the same colours as above and take the pupils' suggestions for the interest levels as the story proceeds – the given graph is a suggested one only.

Group and independent work

Ask each pupil to return to the story opening they wrote yesterday, add in a bit more detail then build in another event where something else goes wrong – a conflict. Demonstrate how to do this.

Differentiation

Low Attainers – Can work with the teacher in a guided writing session where you support them in the next stages of their story.

High Attainers – Plan the rest of their stories using a flow chart on acetate sheets to share with the class.

Whole class

Ask several of the high attaining group to outline their plans using the OHT.

Lesson 4

Whole class

For variety, devote the whole of this literacy hour to an extended writing session.

Ask each pupil to re-read what they have done so far, then plan on a separate piece of paper how their story will continue. Expect them to build in one more complication and development before their stories are resolved.

Differentiation

Low Attainers – Can follow the individual guidance given yesterday.

High Attainers – Can finish their stories, checking the structure against the flow charts they prepared yesterday.

Lesson 5

Whole class

Again, use this whole session for giving time for all pupils to finish, then proof-read and edit, their stories; make sure that they check any more dialogue they have written for the correct punctuation.

At the end of this extended writing session, collect their books in and mark for:

- correct punctuation of dialogue
- story structure and pace – mark the complications in red and the developments in green.

Comment in a very focused way on these two objectives.

If either is weak, ask them to work on one section of the story to improve on these two objectives.

Theme 5) Fiction characters in stories

Objectives

Text level
- 3 to investigate how characters are presented, referring to the text:
  - through dialogue, action and description
  - how the reader responds to them
  - through examining their relationships with other characters
- 9 to develop an active attitude towards reading
- 15 to write new scenes or characters into a story in the manner of the writer
- 3 & 6 proof-reading and attention to punctuation as in previous fiction unit
- 7 how to set out dialogue

Resources
Copies of *James and the Giant Peach* by Roald Dahl; ask pupils to bring in their own copies and library copies.
Copies of *A Stack of Story Poems* by Tony Bradman.
A collection of Year R reading scheme books which have no text and/or picture books with the text covered.
Group reading books currently being used.
Suggested OHT extracts for whole class sessions from the Dahl book as follows:

Chapter 2, 2nd and 3rd paragraphs: 'It all started ... at her own hideous face'.
Chapter 13, near the beginning of the chapter 'For goodness sake. Stop staring round the room ... It's time for bed'.
Whiteboards and pens.
Copymasters 8 and 9: clue cards – Copymaster 8: Appearance of character; actions; how he/she feels. Copymaster 9: What author wants you to feel.
Homework 5.

Assessment
At the end of this theme is the pupil able to:
- analyse the way writers can influence readers to take a particular view of characters, both positive and negative;
- become more active readers through visualising scenes, empathising with characters, predicting next events and solving puzzles in the text through discussion and reflection;
- through close scrutiny of the author's style, write another paragraph which mirrors the way in which the author develops character;
- write a piece of dialogue and punctuate it accurately?

Lesson 1

Whole class

Explain that the objectives of this unit are to study closely how writers can influence readers to form opinions on character – the challenge is to become 'detective readers' who can work out what the author is trying to do, and how he/she achieves this.
Put up the first OHT you have prepared from Chapter 2 of *James and the Giant Peach*.
Read it, then divide the class into 3 sections and ask them to be 'detective readers' for clues to Dahl's opinion of James, Aunt Sponge or Aunt Spiker.
Give the class 2 minutes to write down what they think with reference to the text.
Write down their ideas under the characters' names.
Now put up the second extract from Chapter 13 and this time divide the class up into 2 halves – do the same for James and the Centipede.

Group and independent work
Hand out copies of *James and the Giant Peach* and ask pupils to turn to Chapter 12.
Ask pupils to choose an insect character (Centipede, Earthworm, Ladybird, Miss Spider, Old Green Grasshopper), write down his/her name: and write down what they note about the character.

Differentiation
Low Attainers – Can work on two selected characters only.
High Attainers – Comment on style/choice of words and how Dahl is manipulating the reader's views.

Whole class
Refer to the original list and add more detail to the profile of James and the Centipede – what is Dahl's aim in these portrayals?

Lesson 2

Whole class

Ask pupils to bring their work to this session and share what they wrote in the previous lesson about the characters. Ask them how Dahl colours their attitude to each of these characters. *e.g. through his choice of adjectives to describe appearance or verbs and adverbs to describe how the character speaks and/or acts.*
Now model how to write in the style of Dahl by writing as a boastful butterfly, using the conversation between the Earthworm and the Centipede at the beginning of Chapter 12 as a model.

Group and independent work
Ask pupils in pairs to produce a piece of dialogue between the Ladybird and the Earthworm where the

Ladybird copies the style of the Centipede's boasts, talking about her appearance and skills.

Differentiation
Low Attainers – Write a piece of dialogue where the Aunts call James 'a disgusting little beast' from Chapter 1 of the book. Give them a dialogue frame to write this in.
High Attainers – Write a piece of dialogue in which Miss Spider tells the Grasshopper and the Ladybird where their beds are.
Then get them to compare their dialogue with the real thing. How close were they to the predicted style?

Whole class
Ask the high attaining group to feed back on the similarities and differences between their text and Dahl's

Lesson 3

This session will start off with the group session first, followed by a whole class presentation.

Group work

Display the Rules for Dialogue Poster from the previous unit.

Ask the whole class, in pairs, to proof-read and check the accuracy in punctuation of their piece of dialogue from yesterday.

Then pupils should write a comment on how their piece of dialogue mirrors Dahl's style.

Finally, each pair should rehearse their piece of dialogue orally in preparation for a presentation to the whole class.

Whole class

One pupil from each pair explains how their piece of dialogue mirrors Dahl's style. They then perform their dialogue.

E.g.

Summarise Dahl's style and technique:
• argumentative
• exclamation marks
• italics for emphasis
• powerful verbs
• strong adjectives

Lesson 4

Whole class

Read aloud *Bandanna Billy* by Kaye Umansky, *Benny McEever* by Gareth Owen or any other story poem, stopping at significant points to take pupils' views on: what might happen next; attitudes/appearance towards a character so far; what the author wants you to feel.

Group and independent work

Ask groups of pupils to use the clue cards from Copymasters 8 and 9 to make notes on:

Side 1: appearance/actions of character.
Side 2: what the author wants you to feel.
Use a story, poem or chapter from a book they are reading as a group in order to fill in the clue cards.

Differentiation

Low and *High Attainers* use appropriate materials for the same activities as the rest of the class.

Whole class

Ask two groups to reflect on what they have learned about the author's portrayal of characters.

Lesson 5

Whole class

Show two reading scheme books with no text which have a storyline centred on characters' behaviour.
Ask the class how the author is able to convey characters' feelings without text.
Ask pupils to give you ideas for writing a piece of dialogue between two of the characters. Develop the dialogue through shared writing.

Independent work

Using one book each, if possible, or one between two, ask pupils to write a piece of dialogue which conveys the feeling of the characters as shown by the illustrations. After each line of dialogue, pupils must check the accuracy of their punctuation. Collect books in and discuss with the class, talking particularly about punctuation and characterisation.

Differentiation

Low Attainers – Can be asked for a shorter piece of dialogue.
High Attainers – Write in another scene for the story and then produce notes for the illustrator on how the characters must look and act – their facial expressions act as the unspoken text.

Whole class

Ask the class what they enjoyed most in this unit, and what they have learned.

Theme 6) Book reviews

Objectives

Text level

- 4 to consider how texts can be rooted in the writer's experience
- 10 to evaluate a book by referring to details and examples in the text
- 12 to discuss the enduring appeal of established authors
- 13 to record ideas, reflections and predictions about a book

Resources

A favourite book of yours to use for demonstration purposes at the beginning of the lesson.
A favourite book which pupils have brought into school or borrowed from the classroom bookshelf or library.
Some 'classic' books.
The Butterfly Lion by Michael Morpurgo.
Whiteboards and pens.
Copymaster 10 – The book I really like – and why.
Copymaster 11 – 'Blurbs' on an A4 sheet.
Homework 6.

Assessment

At the end of this theme is the pupil able to:

- explain and justify his/her views regarding his/her favourite writers;
- understand, through the study of text and information on authors, how real life experiences can often be used in books?

Lesson 1

Whole class

Explain that the focus of this unit is about how important it is to discuss and work out just why certain books appeal to us and be able to quote from the book to show what we mean.
Use Copymaster 10 as an OHT. Fill this in with the class, referring to your book.
Read out the quotes and say why you chose those particular ones, e.g. *I chose this paragraph because it builds up a really creepy picture of what's about to happen; I chose this piece of dialogue because it shows how much one character hated the other!*

Group and independent work

Give out the same evaluation sheet to each pupil.
Ask pupils to skim through the first chapter of their favourite book, looking for quotes that they might use.

Next, they must read through, but not fill in, the same evaluation sheet.

Differentiation

All groups follow the same activity, with books which match their appeal and interest.

Whole class

Ask pupils to arrange themselves in a circle, and ask one pupil from each group to present their book to the group, 'talking' to Copymaster 10 filled in rather than reading it out.
They must quote from the text at least once.
In preparation for tomorrow's literacy hour, put up a list of the following authors: Enid Blyton, Roald Dahl, Anne Fine, Judy Blume, Susan Cooper, C.S. Lewis, J.R.R. Tolkein, Joan Aiken, Rosemary Sutcliffe, Philippa Pearce, Robert Westall. Ask if pupils have read books by any of them. If pupils have the books, ask them to bring them in; otherwise, find some of them in school.

Lesson 2

Whole class

This lesson is linked to the notion of the 'enduring appeal' of some authors.
Make sure this session lasts a full half hour: pupils love the time to gossip about writers and books they love!
Refer to the display of books which pupils have brought in (some of these books are likely to be the same ones they brought in for yesterday's lesson).

Group work

Divide pupils into manageable author groups to discuss between them just what makes these books equally attractive to yesterday's, today's and tomorrow's readers.
Ask each group to come up with a list of the most important reasons why some books are loved across the generation gap. Produce a list of your own and share it with the pupils.

Whole class

Each group shares its list with the class. Discuss any common features.

Lesson 3

Whole class

Explain that this lesson is linked to the idea that texts can be rooted in a writer's real experience.

Explain that many writers are listening in to other people's conversations; reading up on a subject they know little about; thinking about what happened to them in the past; watching people's behaviour. Many writers build into their books some aspect of what they have seen, heard, read or experienced.

Say that you will give out a collection of 'blurbs' (Copymaster 11) and the task is to predict whether the writer could have actually experienced these things or has read about them. (The correctness of these opinions is not important, but the quality of the discussion is.)

Group and independent task

In pairs, pupils read these blurbs, and decide what evidence they can find. If there is no evidence, what are they to assume?

Differentiation

Low attainers – Read blurbs which they have no difficulty reading

High attainers – Select their own blurbs and justify their views.

Whole class

One group shares and justifies their views and discusses the purpose of blurbs.

Lesson 4

Whole class

Make an OHP of the preface to *The Butterfly Lion* by Michael Morpurgo. Display this on the OHT throughout the reading of the book.

As you read the book ask pupils to jot down ideas, reflections, predictions and any connections with the OHT preface in front of them.

Stop approximately every 15 minutes and give them 2 minutes to do this and then share their ideas.

Read the book during the next two lessons.

Lesson 5

Divide the class up into 6 different groups and give each group one of the questions from the list below, as well as the name of the character.

Explain that each group will go into role as a character, and a pupil will pose the question on the card.

Pupils can decide to add in other questions, beginning with 'How did you feel when.......?

What did you learn about....? What are your feelings now about....?

Give them 5 minutes to discuss it.

Key characters	Typical questions
Bertie as a young boy in Africa	Why were you so interested in the waterhole?
Bertie's father	Why did you allow Bertie to keep the lion?
Bertie's mother	Tell us how you felt when Bertie left for England.
Millie as a young girl	What did you like about Bertie?
Millie as the old lady	What was it like, having a lion to look after?
The young boy who runs away from school	Was the old lady real, or a ghost?

Role-play is a powerful learning tool for understanding characters in books, and underlying themes.

Finally, ask pupils what messages they think the author was trying to give readers (theme).

Theme 7) Non-fiction

Objectives

Text level
- 22 to read and evaluate a range of instructional texts in terms of their purpose, organisation and layout and clarity and usefulness
- 25 to write instructional texts and test them out

Sentence level
- 8 to revise and extend work on verbs, focusing on tense, form and person
- 9 to identify the imperative form in instructional writing

Resources
Collections of recipes/DIY instructions/games

instructions brought in by pupils, including those for software.
Copymaster 12 – Recipes.
Copymaster 13 – Pancakes.
Homework 7.

Assessment
At the end of this theme is the pupil able to:
- read and evaluate the clarity, usefulness, purpose and organisation of instructional texts;
- write instructional texts and test them out;
- revise the use of verbs in instructional texts and use appropriately, including the use of the imperative form?

Lesson 1

Whole class

Explain the objectives of this unit to pupils, saying that they are going to read, analyse and write instructional texts and, more importantly, try out their instructions on someone else to see if they are clear to the person reading them.

Group/pair work
In order to assess their experience of using instructions, ask each group to work in pairs.
Ask each pair to discuss and jot down the kinds of instructions they use in their own lives.

Group and independent work
Then ask the children to choose a subject, e.g. *instructions for playing badminton plaiting hair* and practise miming the activity.
Can the rest of the class guess what they are doing?
Now demonstrate how to write instructions for one of the mimed activities. Ask the children to make some suggestions.
Note the verbs used – explain that this is the imperative form. Instructions tell you what to do.

Whole class
Ask the class what they have learned in this literacy hour and give them 1 minute to discuss this in pairs.
List the children's responses.

Lesson 2

Whole class

Ask the children to tell you what they know about the language features of instructions. List their responses.
Show children an example of instructions, *e.g. a recipe*.
Ask what tense it is written in – past, present or future. Establish that it is the present tense – establish that this is because it is happening now.
Ask whether it is written in any kind of order – establish that it is in time order (chronological).
Introduce the mnemonic PAT (Present tense, Active, Time order).

Group and independent work
Hand out a selection of texts which have had all the imperative verbs deleted (for example, Copymaster 12). Ask the class, in pairs, to work out the missing words and write them in their books.

Differentiation
Low Attainers – Cut up some instructions and ask pupils to re-order them.
High Attainers – Give the children a set of instructions with missing words (e.g. Copymaster 13). Children can identify the missing elements by reading the rest of the instructions, using the clues or looking up a set of similar instructions in a book or on the Internet.

Whole class
Give out copies of the same recipes from the Copymasters which you have completed. Ask pupils to swap them with another pair to check how well they have done in replacing the missing words.
Ask for feedback on how well they have done and what they have learned.

Lesson 3

Whole class

Take the class to the outside play area or to the gym. Have ready small and large apparatus and ask pupils in mixed ability groups to plan a new team game (15 minutes).

Using clip boards, a scribe for the team writes down their instructions for playing the game. These may be accompanied by a diagram.

Each group then swaps their instructions with a different group and tries out that game.

Ask each group to decide on the marks out of 10 they will give to the writer of the instructions, and feed back some detailed comments.

Lesson 4–5

Group and independent work

Linking the literacy hour to other curricular areas (e.g. D and T, Art, Science), ask pupils to produce a set of instructions in Lesson 4, then try them out on a friend in Lesson 5 (this may be as a form of revision in any subject area).

Expect that they will incorporate some of the suggestions for improvement in their instructions noted from Lesson 3's feedback.

Each pupil must write an evaluation on a post-it note and stick it on their friend's instructions.

Whole class

Ask for one person from each group to say what they now know about instructions. Ensure that they fully understand the purpose, structure and typical language features.

These could be listed and displayed as a class poster.

Theme 8) Word play and the writing of metaphors

Objectives

Text level
- 8 to investigate and collect different examples of word play, relating form to meaning
- 17 to write metaphors from original ideas or similes

Resources
Michael Rosen's *Book of Nonsense*; *Hairy Tales and Nursery Crimes*; *Walking the Bridge of Your Nose*; any good poetry anthologies; joke books, *e.g. The Schoolkids' Too!*; tongue twisters.
Copymasters 14 and 15.
Picture of a fox and a cobra.

Homework 8. 2 sets of cards. Set 1: Mum, Dad etc. Set 2: Strawberry etc.

Assessment
At the end of this theme is the pupil able to:
- investigate and collect different examples of wordplay from a range of sources;
- identify the use of idiomatic phrases and cliches used in headlines to support effect and wordplay;
- relate form to meaning;
- understand the effect of metaphors as a literary device;
- write his/her own metaphors based on his/her own ideas, using similes as a starting point?

Lesson 1

Whole class

Explain to the class that they will be finding out how poets play with words in a variety of different and amusing ways. Explain that the first three lessons of the week will focus on writers playing with words.
Start by asking them if they can remember any tongue twisters, and ask a few volunteers to say them to the class.
Then give some examples of jokes which play on words, *e.g. What did the hat say to the scarf? You hang around and I'll go on ahead! What did Cinderella say to the photographer? Some day my prints will come!* Write these examples and more that you can find in front of the pupils.
Get them to explain why they are funny. Which words are crucial for the jokes to work?
Ask pupils to come up with some more jokes they know that play on words and share them with the class.

Group or independent work
Have ready collections of joke books, headlines from sports pages, comics with joke sections, advertisements from glossy magazines and jingles, *e.g. Go to Work on an Egg; Naughty but Nice; Have a Break, Have a Kit Kat!*
Ask pupils to investigate the collections and write down examples they like, and explain why.

Differentiation
Low Attainers – Prepare a group presentation of a selection of jokes which they find funny.
High Attainers – By studying the play on words in the sports headlines, make up their own sports headlines.

Whole class
The low attaining group should present their jokes; the rest of the class write the word or words which make(s) the joke funny.

Lesson 2

Whole class

Show pupils the examples on Copymaster 15 where Michael Rosen has played around with nursery rhymes to make them funnier.
Then show them the tongue twister on *Fried Fish*.
In each case, ask them to explain how they work.
Model how to change an ending using *Humpty Dumpty*: ask pupils to make a list of rhyming words for 'men', choose a word and make up an ending.
Get them to do the same for their own rhyme (good rhymes to use are *Simple Simon* or *Jack Be Nimble*).

Group or independent work
Ask pupils in pairs to produce an alternative ending to a nursery rhyme from those suggested above.

Differentiation
Low Attainers – In pairs, read a selection of other examples from one of Rosen's books, choose one and write down what they like about it.
High Attainers – Write a different version of the *Fried Fish* poem. Ask pupils to work together in pairs and produce a new tongue twister like *Fried Fish*, *e.g. Big Baked Beans, Sautéed Sizzling Salmon*.

Whole class
Choose one of the groups who have worked on a nursery rhyme. Ask each pair to explain how they went about this task, what was hard and what was easy, then read out what they have written so far.

Lesson 3

Whole class

Display the three examples of concrete poems (Copymaster 14) and ask three different pupils to read each out.
After each poem, ask the class to explain what they liked about it and how the shape of the poem linked to the meaning.

Group or independent work

Using the caterpillar poem as a model, ask pupils in pairs to produce a mind-map of words for a concrete poem of their own.

Differentiation

Low Attainers – Could be given a selection of words to start their brainstorm off.
High Attainers – Could be challenged to write a poem based on a sloth, where they would have to research information on a sloth, make a mind-map of words then decide on a suitable outline to represent its immobility!

Whole class

Give each group 2 minutes to talk about what they understand by the term 'wordplay'.

Lesson 4

Whole class

Explain that in this lesson, the pupils are going to do some work on similes because these help to spice up both poetry and fiction writing, creating pictures in readers' heads.
Explain that a simile is a suggestion that one thing is like another.
Show some examples: *as hard as nails, as green as grass, as cold as ice, as playful as a kitten.* Ask for any others which they know.
Now introduce the simile which moves closer to a metaphor: *She was trembling like a leaf; The kite rose like a bird.* Explain that these similes compare a person or an object to a different thing – underline **she** and draw an arrow to **leaf**; underline **kite** and draw an arrow to **bird**.
Reveal four more examples: *The grey playground was like a huge yawn; The motorway was like a twisting snake; The tulip was like an open smile; The cat was like a warm cushion.*

Ask different pupils to tell you which words to underline and where to draw the arrow.

Group or independent work

Display the pictures of the fox and the camel.
Ask each pupil to choose one animal and write 3 similes for different parts of the animal's body: FOX – ears, eyes, nose, tail, whole animal; COBRA – marks, eyes, ribs, tail, whole animal.

Differentiation

Low Attainers – Prepare a simple frame for the fox: *His ears are like tall ...; His eyes are like flashing ...; His tail is like a bushy ...* then ask them to prepare one for the whole animal: *The fox is like a ...*
High Attainers – As the rest of the class, differentiated by outcome.

Whole class

Suspend this session, and use pupils' ideas as the basis for moving into metaphor at the beginning of tomorrow's lesson. Collect their work in and copy out some of their ideas.

Lesson 5

Whole class

Show pupils' some of their ideas from yesterday's lesson and re-state that these are similes.
State that a metaphor says that one thing *is* another.
Delete the word 'like' from their ideas, turning them into metaphors: *His ears are tall listening posts; His eyes are flashing signals; His tail is a bushy brush.*
Show some examples of metaphors from real poets.
Demonstrate writing some of your own: *The moon is an icy maiden; the sun is a raging furnace; the stars are priceless jewels.*

Group or independent work

Give each group two sets of cards: *Mum, Dad, sister, brother, Gran, auntie, me* (set 1) and *strawberry, apple, lemon, peach, sunny, rainy, stormy, grey* (set 2).
Taking it in turns, one member of the group takes a card from set 1 and one from set 2.
Another member must act as scribe and write down their contributions.
The card chooser must say a metaphor, e.g. *My gran is a sour lemon; My brother is a sunny day.*

Differentation

Low Attainers and *High Attainers* are placed in mixed ability groups and share their ideas.

Whole class

The scribe in each group reads out their ideas. Ask for comments on particularly effective metaphors in order to reflect on learning.

Theme 9) Comparing two different poets

Objectives

Text level
- 6 to read a number of poems by significant poets and identify what is distinctive about the style or content of their poems
- 7 to analyse and compare poetic style, use of forms and the themes of significant poets; to respond to shades of meaning; to explain and justify personal tastes; to consider the impact of full rhymes, half rhymes, internal rhymes and other sound patterns
- 16 to convey feelings, reflections or moods in a poem through the careful selection of words and phrases

Word level
- 7 to explain the differences between synonyms and to collect, classify and order sets of words to identify shades of meaning

Resources
Copies of these poems by Hillaire Belloc: *Rebecca; Jack and His Pony, Tom* (Copymasters 16 and 17) and James Reeves' *Spells* and *The Intruder* (Copymaster 18). Enlarged OHT versions of the above poems. Homework 9.

Assessment
At the end of this theme is the pupil able to:
- analyse and compare the poetic style and content of two poets;
- explain and justify personal tastes;
- consider the impact of rhyme and other sound patterns;
- convey feelings, reflections or moods through the careful selection of words or phrases;
- identify shades of meaning through collecting, classifying and ordering synonyms?

Lesson 1

Whole class
Explain to the class that in this unit of lessons they are going to compare poems by two different poets, identifying the particular style of each poet. They will all write a poem, and look at shades of meaning in words, during the Synonym Challenge at the end of the week. Display one poem, in italics for emphasis, from each of the poets, using the prepared OHT.
Ask pupils to divide a page into two halves.
Read the poems out aloud. After each poem ask the class to jot down any ideas, emotions or reactions which have occurred during the readings.
Choose six different pupils and ask them to read aloud what they have written. Write captions on card to represent their ideas. Tell pupils to keep their pages for group work.

Group or independent work
In pairs, ask pupils to read each poem on Copymasters 16, 17 and 18 again silently them share their initial reaction. Ask them to jot down some more of their ideas.

Now ask each pair to choose their preferred poem and prepare and rehearse a reading aloud of the poem.

Differentiation
Low Attainers – Give them some statements or questions about the poem written down on card – use the Homework Sheet for ideas. Ask them to discuss these, e.g. Who is the poem about? Does it rhyme? If so, write down some of the rhyming words. How does the poem make you feel? Can you learn anything from the poem?
High Attainers – Ask them for the theme of each poem and a rating of 1–10 on how effective the poet was in supporting that theme, justifying their views with reference to the poem.

Whole class
Fix the captions from the shared session onto a large sheet of paper.
Choose two groups to give feedback on their ideas, grouping their answers under the captions, if applicable, or writing new captions.
Do not choose a high attaining group – use their ideas tomorrow as part of the first shared session.

Lesson 2

Whole class
Explain that the class will decide which poem they prefer; then you will discuss theme and style. Ask pupils to write down 1 or 2 to denote which poem they preferred and to hold up their papers. Count the number of 1s and 2s and share this.
Choose six pairs of pupils to explain and justify their preferences and to read their poem aloud.
Ask the high ability group to share their ideas on the themes of these poems. List these and encourage comments from the class.
Say that their preferences were based on style or theme and content (even if they did not know this).
Display a set of poetry 'style' cards from Homework 9 and run through them.

Group and independent work
Give out two complete sets of cards to each of the groups – one set between three pupils – and small versions of these two poems.
Specify which poet each group must focus on.
Place the cards in the middle of the table and ask pupils to turn over a card and agree if this feature is present in the poem. If so, place it in a 'yes' pile.
Carry on through as many cards as possible. Children record their findings.

Differentiation
Low Attainers – Sort a set of style cards which match the poem. Ask them to find an example of each style feature and highlight it in the poem.
High Attainers – Prepare a presentation to the class where one child in each trio holds up a style card and the other two quote an example.

Whole class
High and low attaining groups present their findings as outlined above, saying what they learned about the author's style.

Lesson 3

Whole class

Tell the class to bring their books from the day before. Display the other two poems but cover the poet's name. Read both poems, then ask the class to vote on which poem matched which poet.

Get them to skim quickly through their notes and see if the same features of style are present in these new poems.

Choose six pupils to talk about what they have noticed.

Group and independent work

Ask the children to choose one of the poets then draft a brief letter, explaining why they enjoyed the poems.

Explain that you will collect in the draft letter, marking it for every text reference they include. Provide a simple frame if necessary to get them on task quickly.

Differentiation

Low Attainers – Give pupils a more detailed writing frame for their letter.

High Attainers – Write an imaginary letter from the poet to readers, explaining the purpose of the poem and the choice of particular words, phrases and other features of style.

Whole class

Ask a selection of children to explain how they went about this task, what they found easy and what they found difficult.

Lesson 4

Whole class

Explain that you will show the class how to write a poem to convey a particular mood.

Choose three style cards. Now select a mood, e.g. 'sad'. The cards will form the basis of a modelled poem, e.g. *variety of length of lines, questions, repetition*.

Place these where pupils can see them. Model how to write this poem, using the structure below if you wish.

Sad

Why was I feeling so low?

Sad and depressed and grey, the long day stretching out in front of me.

Why was I feeling so low?

Sad and depressed and grey, my face in the mirror told its own story.

Group or independent work

Ask pupils in pairs to write two or three more verses.

Differentiation

Low Attainers – Give pupils a partly written poem with some missing words, and ask them to complete it.

High Attainers – Build in another 'style' card, and ask them to draft a few verses.

Whole class

Choose several pupils to read out their lines of the new poem, explaining how they match the style cards.

Lesson 5

Whole class

Synonym Challenge!

Explain that poets choose words very carefully: they have a thesaurus in their heads!

Explain that in groups pupils will be given ten minutes to use thesauruses to look up this list and find different synonyms: *Hungry, livid, incessant, glorious, unhappy.*

Write the synonyms on pieces of paper.

Set a timer to run for 10 minutes.

Finally ask pupils to arrange their words on their tables in order of effect, or shades of meaning.

Group or independent work

Ask each pupil to finish writing up to three verses of their poem.

Swap it with a partner, read it, and write comments on post-it notes.

Give it back to the partner and explain the comments (two good points, one constructive point).

Differentiation

Low Attainers – Complete the poem from yesterday, then add in one new verse.

High Attainers – Research other work by their preferred poet on the Internet or by using their school library to find other poems.

Whole class

Ask each group to come up with a reflection on one thing they learned from this theme of work.

Theme 10 Word order

Objectives

Sentence level

* 1 to investigate word order by examining how far the order of words in sentences can be changed:
  * which words are essential to meaning
  * which can be deleted without damaging the basic meaning
  * which words or groups of words can be moved into a different order
* 3 to discuss, proof-read and edit their own writing, creating more complex sentences
* 4 to adapt writing for different readers and purposes, *e.g. younger audiences*
* 6 to understand the need for punctuation as an aid to the reader, *e.g. commas to mark grammatical boundaries; a colon to signal a list*

Resources

A class washing line and pegs.
Copymaster 19 – Examples for pupils to work on.
Copymaster 20 – Preparing for your hamster.
Collections of information books suitable for 6 year olds.
Homework 10.

Assessment

At the end of this theme, is the pupil able to:

* manipulate a sentence around the main clause, both by deleting and moving around groups of words;
* use correct punctuation of colons and commas to separate subordinate clauses;
* design a text which matches audience needs and purpose?

Lesson 1

Whole class

Explain that the objective of the next two lessons is to look at changes we can make to the words in sentences.

Delete and Keep

Illustrate this using the following sentences written as words on individual cards and pegged to a clothes line. Ask children for suggestions as to which words to remove, for example:

1 The black flies, which were hovering over the open dustbin, suddenly moved away.
2 The black flies, which were hovering over the open dustbin, moved away.
3 The black flies, which were hovering, moved away.
4 The flies moved away.

Say that this is the most we can delete to leave a meaningful unit – a sentence that still makes sense.
Tell them that what we keep is called the main clause; you will be returning to this idea in tomorrow's lesson and later in the year.

Group and independent work

Give out the sentences below. Ask pupils to cut them up

then work as a group to remove as many words as they can, leaving a sentence.

The little children played happily on the sandy beach.
The thin lady broke her arm when she tripped over a pile of rubbish.
The grey squirrels chased the greedy blackbirds who were eating their piles of nuts.
The huge seagull, which cried and wheeled in the wind, suddenly fell to earth like a stone.
The young blackbird, startled by the huge magpie, shook with fear.

Differentiation

Low Attainers – Can work on the first two sentences.
High Attainers – Can work on the last two, then design a sentence of their own and cut it up in the same way.

Whole class

Each group takes a different sentence, pegs it on a line, then remove cards in turn, in front of the class. The class agrees whether the remaining sentence (main clause) makes sense and still keeps the basic meaning of the original sentence.

Lesson 2

Whole class

This lesson is another active one in which pupils work out which groups of words can be moved around in sentences. Demonstrate this by using Copymaster 19: each sentence has the main clause underlined. Now display each sentence on a washing line and ask pupils to come and move a section around.
When each sentence has been worked on, ask them if they notice any common things about this group of words they have moved around (each bit is an adverbial phrase describing 'how' or 'where').
Ask if the sentences have been improved in any way *e.g. does the sentence about the watch read better?*

Group or independent activities

Ask pairs to finish off a sentence with an adverbial phrase, write it on cards then place it on a washing line. Here are some suggestions for beginnings: *The green snake slithered ... ; The old man hobbled ... ; Tom moved ... ; Tara worked ... ; The flowers swayed ...*

Differentiation

Low Attainers – Can work on the first two sentences.
High Attainers – Can work on the last two, then design a sentence of their own and cut it up in the same way.

Whole class

Each group allows their sentence to be worked on by the rest of the class.

Lesson 3

Whole class

The aim of this lesson is to focus on the use of commas to separate subordinate clauses (which will support later work on complex sentences) and the use of colons.
Use the examples from Lesson 1 (the flies, seagull and blackbird sentences) to demonstrate how the commas separate the subordinate clause and then get the class to suggest some more: *Aunt Spiker, ..., rushed over to James. The centipede, ..., scurried over to the earthworm.*
Now give an example of the use of the colon (to introduce a list): *The house included the following: a lounge, a new kitchen, three large bedrooms and an indoor swimming pool.* Leave these models up for the next activity.

Independent work

Ask some pupils to choose any well-known character from a book they have read and write 3 sentences. Each must start with the character's name followed by a comma, then some more information followed by a comma, then the sentence must be finished off. *E.g. John, my brother's best friend, loved chips.* Ask other pupils to empty their school bags and write a sentence using a colon followed by the contents of the bag, e.g. *In my bag were:*

Differentiation

Low Attainers – Write another colon sentence e.g. *in my desk were:.*
High Attainers – Write 3 non-fiction sentences linked to the class history or geography topic, using subordinate clauses.

Whole class

Ask some children to write up their sentences. Other children can underline the main clause in one colour and the subordinate clause in another. Ask children to check for the correct use of commas. Try reading the sentences without the commas. Discuss how this makes them more difficult to understand.

Lesson 4

Whole class

Explain to the class that the next two lessons will again have a spotlight on sentences and on the layout of an information text for a 6-year-old.

Group work

When pupils are in groups, explain to the class the task above, then tell each group to skim read some books for 6 year olds to see how the layout and sentence structure are chosen for younger children. Give them 10 minutes to jot down some ideas.

Whole class

Ask the class to share their ideas and write up a list of advice (simple sentences, lots of illustrations and photographs, interesting layout, use of colour etc.).
Now show them Copymaster 20. The purpose of the text is to offer advice on a suitable home for a hamster and the audience is a 6-year-old. Ask for pupils' views as to its suitability; ask them to jot down ideas in 30 seconds.
Add any other advice to the list already made.

Independent work

Ensure that each pupil has a copy of this text, which they should annotate to make an action plan for change. e.g., 1st heading: buying a cage, 2nd heading: what to put inside the cage, 3rd heading: what hamsters eat in the cage, 4th heading: how hamsters exercise in the cage.

Differentiation

This will be through outcome for all individual pupils.

Whole class

Ask selected pupils to share some of their action plans and notes.

Lesson 5

This is used as an extended session in order to complete the whole task.
The work will be collected in and marked for audience and purpose.

As a final evaluation, a group of 6-year-olds could be invited to the class to comment on the advice sheet, or the sheet could be sent to infant pupils for their comments.

Theme 1) Poems

Objectives

Text level

- 4 to read a range of narrative poems
- 5 to perform poems in a variety of ways
- 6 to understand terms which describe different sorts of poems
- 10 to understand the differences between literal and figurative language
- 12 to use the structure of poems read to write extensions based on these

Resources

A set of cards with poetry types already met in the framework, *e.g. haiku, epitaphs, rhyming poems, rap, ballads and narrative poems.*

Copymaster 21 – *Nettles* by Vernon Scannell. Homework 11.
Selection of narrative and rap poems from Big Books or anthologies.

Assessment

At the end of this theme is the pupil able to:
- read a range of narrative poems;
- perform poems in a variety of ways;
- understand terms which describe different sorts of poems;
- understand the differences between literal and figurative language;
- use the structure of poems read to write extensions?

Lesson 1

Whole class

Show the cards and ask if pupils recognise these terms, giving a example of a poem in this category; if not, give the definition using an adult dictionary. Place these in the space allocated for ongoing literacy work, or on a class washing line.

Explain that they will be looking in particular at narrative poems and ballads in this theme.

This lesson will be about narrative poems. Ask if they have heard the term 'narrative' before (linked to story structure) – say that narrative poems tell a story. Read an OHT or enlarged version of *The Listeners* by Walter de la Mare, asking the class to think about what happens in this poem. Using their suggestions, make a flow chart to represent the events in the poem.

Ask a pupil to volunteer to be the Traveller, and to voice his thoughts when he/she gets no response.

Say that the poem is mostly using literal language, *e.g.*

the horse champed (chewed) the grasses; a bird flew out of the turret ie. What a actually happens.

Group and independent work

Hand out copies of another narrative poem, *e.g. The Train to Glasgow by Wilma Horsbrugh*, and ask pupils to make a flow chart of events. Ask one pupil to tell the story to his/her friend.

Differentiation

Low Attainers – Need to have had *The Train to Glasgow* read to them, possibly as part of a guided reading session the week before.

High Attainers – Can work on *Nettles* by Vernon Scannell (Copymaster 21). Ask them to spot the metaphors then prepare a dramatic version of it, in mime only, with two characters: the 3 year old and his father.

Whole class

Ask 3 pairs of pupils to tell the story of the poem. Now read the poem to them again. Do they prefer their version or the poem? Ask children to justify their reasons.

Lesson 2

Whole class

Start off this session by using 2 members of yesterday's group to perform a mime version of what happened in *Nettles*. Ask the rest of the class to make a few guesses about what had happened.

Display an enlarged version of *Nettles*. Read it to the class and ask them for the story within the poem; ask them how well the mime scene told the story. Say that so far only literal language has been used in the poems, but this group are about to underline some metaphors or figurative language. Before they do, challenge the class to identify some!

Then use members of the *high attaining* group to underline all the figurative language found in it (*green spears, fierce parade, funeral pyre, fallen dead, tall recruits, sharp wounds* – war/battle metaphors).

Group and independent work

Hand out another narrative, *e.g. the poem Colonel Fazackerley by Charles Causley*, and ask each group to write a flow chart of events.

Whole class

After 15 minutes, tell the class that you are going to rehearse, as a class, a choral reading of the poem. Get boys and girls reading alternate verses.

This could be used as part of an assembly presentation.

Lesson 3

Whole class

The Highwayman – 1

Read *The Highwayman* by Alfred Noyes and ask pupils to jot down any metaphors/similes as examples of figurative language: *e.g. wind = torrent of darkness; moon = ghostly galleon; Tim's eyes = hollows of darkness; his hair = mouldy hay.*

Ask the class for a quick summary of events and write these down in a bullet point list. They will need this for lesson 4.

Group and independent work

Give out copies of the poem and ask each group to prepare notes for interviews by you.

Interview in turn: the Highwayman, Bess, Tim, King George's men. Allocate different characters to different groups.

Differentiation

Low Attainers – Prepare a list of notes for Bess, with some gaps for them to fill in.

High Attainers – Write down a piece of imagined dialogue between Bess and the Highwayman in the after life.

Whole class

Interview each group in turn, the whole group answering in role as one character (except for King George's men).

Lesson 4

Whole class

The Highwayman – 2

Tell the class that they are going to take the main events of this poem and turn it into a rap.
Read out some raps from a Big Book.
Ask them to say or sing raps they know, and clap their hands in time to the beat.
Start them off through modelled writing, using the following lines, if you wish.

The weather was bad
But he was feeling good!
He was dressed to kill
But he wanted his fill –
Of Bess, Bess,

His darling Bess.

Group and independent work

Referring to the bullet point list of events you wrote yesterday, ask the class to start preparing a rap, in pairs.

Differentiation

Low Attainers – Can continue this rap; give them the events they must include.

High Attainers – Can complete the rap as for the rest of the class.

Whole class

Ask any pupils if they are ready to give a 'taster' of their rap to the class and to tell the class what they found hard about this task.

Lesson 5

Whole class

The class will continue writing the raps including proof-reading and editing them ready for *The New Rap Version of The Highwayman by Class ——*.

Make time for each pair to perform their rap to the rest of the class.

Theme 2) Oral storytelling

Objectives

Text level
- 3 to explore similarities and differences between oral and written storytelling
- 14 to make notes of story outline as preparation for oral storytelling

Resources
Traditional stories, including fairy tales. Any collections of myths, fables and legends.
Copymaster 22 – Cinderella: example of written and oral storytelling.

Copymaster 23 – Guidelines for a storyteller.
Homework 12.

Assessment
At the end of this theme is the pupil able to:
- select key events from a story in the form of notes and tell it;
- keep to the story line and characterisation of the original writing;
- add the storyteller's 'magic'?

Lesson 1

Whole class

Explain to the class that this unit is about storytelling. This is because traditional stories like fairy stories, myths, fables and legends were originally spoken, rather than written: the majority of people could not write and had to memorise these stories. Many would have been told them as children but even when they were adults, stories were still told to them. Before television, radio and books, and for hundreds of years after print was invented, storytelling was the major way in which people entertained themselves.

As we learnt in last week's unit, stories were a useful way of passing on ideas of how to handle the big issues in life such as jealousy and hatred: fables were very useful indeed for giving adults and children a 'code of conduct' on how to behave.

Read the opening section of *Cinderella*, the children following on an OHT or an enlarged version.

Now **tell** the opening part of the fairy story and asks pupils what the differences are between the two. Show Copymaster 23 – Guidelines for a storyteller – and say that pupils should use this as a useful checklist when preparing their own stories for telling.

Group and independent work
Give each group your notes for the rest of the story, including the feelings of the characters.
Ask pupils in turn to rehearse the next section of the story in their groups, making the story come alive. They do not have to learn the written story off by heart! Give each group a copy of Copymaster 23.

Defferentiation
All groups work on the same task.

Whole class
Ask each group to tell a section at a time, the rest of the class saying what was effective about the storytelling techniques.

Lesson 2

Whole class

Display Copymaster 23 again, and tell the class that today they must make their own notes from a story in preparation for the telling of it.

Group and independent work
Ask pupils to group and read a well known fairy story, e.g. *The Three Little Pigs, Cinderella, Golidlocks and the Three Bears, Sleeping Beauty,* and ask them to prepare notes on cards.
Ask them to rehearse the telling of the fairy tale in turns, moving around the group. Choose one pupil per

group to make comments on how well the children are storytelling.
Give out small versions of the 'Guidelines for a storyteller' to act as a reference.

Differentiation
Low Attainers – Can have the notes ready prepared.
High Attainers – Use the same approach as the others.

Whole class
Choose two groups to tell their story, the rest of the class responding by using Copymaster 23 to focus on something they did well.

Lesson 3

Whole class

This time the children will base their storytelling on a new story they have not heard before – a myth.
As you read it aloud, ask pupils to jot down the main events of the myth as notes.
Ask the class to read out their notes in the correct time order and to write these as a bullet point list.

Group and independent work

Give out copies of this story – one between two – and ask pupils to start rehearsing the telling of the story in

pairs, using the notes and referring to the actual story if they have to.

Differentaiation

Low Attainers – Can be given the notes already and you can work with them on preparing the telling.
High Attainers – Can work on a different story, making notes.

Whole class

This session is used to extend the storytelling preparation – it will be built into tomorrow's lesson.

Lesson 4

Devote the first 30 minutes of this session to finishing the stories in preparation for the storytelling.

Whole class

Choose one pair from every group to tell this myth, pupils as before evaluating their efforts with the Instructions for a storyteller sheet.

Lesson 5

Whole class

Tell the class that Aesop was a very famous storyteller, specialising in fables. Read aloud one of the fables and demonstrate how you write down the key events and then tell it. Because they are so short, the storyteller can expand the story this time, making up details, *e.g. setting/weather, description of animals.*

Group and independent tasks

Hand out a selection of Aesop's fables and get pupils to jot down the key events and also write the moral in

large print/font. Choose short ones, e.g. *The Fawn and Her Mother; The Flies and the Honey Jar; The Fox and the Lion; The Crab and its Mother; The Shepherd Boy and the Wolf.*
Each pupil plans the telling independently for about 10 minutes, then tells the fable to the group, other pupils evaluating how well he/she is telling it.

Whole class

Each pupil tells the fable as Aesop would have, sitting on a box stage where all the pupils can see.
Choose a selection of the best for a Parent's Assembly.
Reflect on the skills of storytelling.

Theme 3) Explanations

Objectives

Text level
• 15 to read a range of explanatory texts, investigating and noting features of impersonal style
• 22 to plan, compose, edit and refine short non-chronological reports and explanatory texts using reading as a source, focusing on clarity, conciseness and impersonal style
• 24 to evaluate their work

Sentence level
•   7 to explore ambiguities that arise from sentence contractions, *e.g. through signs and headlines*

Resources
A collection of explanatory texts from other subject areas, *e.g. science, geography, history.*

A collection of artefacts, *e.g. examples of finished constructions from DT, pieces of art work.*
Key features of explanation texts on cards for a mobile or a wall display; small versions of these on A4 sheets.
Copymaster 24 – Explanations.
Copymaster 25 – How a washing machine works.
Homework 13.

Assessment
At the end of this theme, is the pupil able to:
• read explanatory texts;
• note and talk about key features within these texts and incorporate them in his/her own written texts, evaluating this to check for clarity, conciseness and impersonal style?

Lesson 1

Whole class

Choose an example of an explanatory text which has the following key features:
1 definition which states what the thing or process is;
2 description of parts and how they work;
3 interesting comments/special features;
4 present tense throughout (passive tense may be used).
Have these features ready on cards and written up on a chart. Give out the cards and ask children to identify the features.
Keep on display the text you have used to point out these features.

Group and independent work
This is quite a difficult text type to write, so introduce the writing of one as follows. Ask groups to match these features for an oral report to explain how a lawnmower, shower, washing machine, kettle, dishwasher etc. works. Read out an explanation as follows::

1 *Hairdryers are used to dry hair quickly.*
2 *They need a source of energy such as electricity or a battery. The energy heats an element in the dryer and forces air over it which is then blown out onto the person's hair.*
3 *Hairdryers have changed over time: they used to be large with big hoods which customers had to sit underneath. Nowadays they are small enough to be carried around and can be used to blow-dry hair on a beach, if so wished!*
Give each group a copy of the key features 1–3.

Differentiation
Low Attainers – Can be given a cloze text; ask them to fill in missing words.
High Attainers – Can be expected to relate this to a different explanation of their choice (e.g. *explain a process in art such as sketching in pastels*).

Whole class
Ask the class to have their key features in front of them and listen carefully to the oral explanations. These can then be evaluated by the class.

Lesson 2

Whole class

Read out the explanation of how hairdryers work. Then write it up in front of the children. Talk about:
• the use at the present tense
• avoiding personal pronouns.
Ask pupils to write the oral texts from yesterday, making absolutely certain that the key features are present.
Each of them to write at the bottom of their text:
Checked for Explanation Text Features 1–4.

Underline the present tense verbs in blue and the passive (if they have any) in green. Double-check that no personal pronouns – *us, we, I* – are present.

Differentiation
Whole class works on the task from yesterday. One group works on an OHT which will be used at the beginning of tomorrow's lesson.

Whole class
Ask the class to contribute their views on what was easy and what was difficult.

Lesson 3

Whole class

Show Copymaster 25.
Ask the whole class to comment positively first of all on the features of explanation texts which are present. Hopefully they will spot the inappropriate use of 'My Mum'.
Go on to share the work of the other pupils who produced their work on OHT yesterday.

Group and independent work

Ask the group to swap their explanations with a partner. Each partner evaluates the work by writing comments on post-it notes.
(The group who worked on OHT can start preparing their work for the next two days, which is to write an explanation for a different curriculum area, based on work they are currently doing – see tomorrow's lesson.)

Lessons 4 and 5

Whole class

As final revision for this text type, put up a text extract *e.g. the process of digestion or the adaptability of living things to desert conditions* and bring out the same set of cards. Read the extract aloud, show pupils the cards and ask them to tell you where to place the cards.
Now read and display a second text from a different book and ask them to discuss the text features in pairs. Ask one pair to come to the front and place the cards where they think they should be.

Group and independent work – 2 days' work

All pupils will now work on an explanation linked to a different curriculum area you are working on. This explanation should be based on something from science *e.g. the behaviour of living things, materials, a series circuit,* history *e.g. explain the impact of railways on the local area,* geography *e.g. explain how and why places change* or on artefacts which you have brought into the class from art or technology (explain the ideas for a design). Pupils can refer to their textbooks for relevant facts or use other information *e.g. CD-Rom* relating to these areas. Copy some samples written by the children onto the whiteboard and ask them to comment on the language features.
This work must have been planned in as part of the different curriculum area – not an add-on task.

Whole class

Collect the work and mark it for:
1 correct text features of an explanation;
2 correct factual information.

Theme 4) Punctuation

Objectives

Sentence level

- 5 to use punctuation effectively to signpost meaning in longer and more complex sentences
- 6 to construct sentences in different ways, while retaining meaning, through:
  - combining two or more sentences;
  - re-ordering them;
  - deleting or substituting words;
  - writing them in more telegraphic ways;
- 9 to secure the use of the comma in embedding clauses within sentences

Resources

Copymaster 26 – Writing sentences.
Copymaster 27 – Musical clauses.
Homework 14.

Assessment

At the end of this theme is the pupil able to:
- construct sentences in different ways and improve his/her own writing by using the same techniques;
- add subordinate clauses within a pair of commas, and understand why writers do this;
- understand how writers use punctuation to replace the spoken voice, and improve his/her own writing by doing this?

Lesson 1

Whole class

Explain to the class that the focus of this theme is on sentences, and that what they learn can be used to improve their own writing.

Tell them the challenge today is to combine two or more sentences in different ways.

Write up the following list and ask pupils to read them and think of suitable conjunctions to join both together: *I washed my hands. I ate my meal. I felt very weak. I had been ill. I rinsed my hair. I put on conditioner. The bridge is closed. The wind is at hurricane force.*

Discuss the conjunctions they suggest. Explore whether different ones could have been used within the same sentences.

Write out each of the new sentences and ask if they can re-order each and yet keep the meaning intact, *e.g. I felt very weak because I had been ill = Because I had been ill, I felt weak.* Draw attention to the use and position of commas.

Group and independent work

Give out a selection of sentences and get the pupils to join them, then re-order them (Copymaster 26).

Differentiation

Low Attainers – Are given a collection of conjunctions they can choose from.

High Attainers – Work on combining three sentences and write more examples themselves.

Whole class

Ask some children to read their sentences. Write up a list of conjunctions used. Encourage children to refer to this when writing and add to it when reading.

Lesson 2

Whole class

Explain to the children that the sentences pupils write can sometimes be too long. By deleting or substituting words the sentence can become more effective and more appealing to the reader.

Model this by writing up the following sentence: *The prince stared with an intent gaze into the darkness of the forest which lay in front of him.* Think aloud as you change it to the following: *The prince stared intently into the dark forest ahead.* **Or** *The prince stared intently into the darkness. The forest lay ahead of him.*

Discuss what you have done. Why is it an improvement on the original?

Write up another sentence from Copymaster 26 and ask the class to write a new version.

Ask the class to share what they have written and ask for the one they like best. They must give reasons.

Group and independent work

In pairs, pupils work on improving the remaining sentences from Copymaster 26.

Differentiation

Low Attainers – Work on the following sentences: *The boy walked down the long and hot and dusty and winding road. He saw the beach and then he saw the sea and then he saw the boat and then he saw the monster.*

High Attainers – Can work on the last sentence from Copymaster 26 and improve it, then continue the story line using some short and effective sentences. Provide them with OHTs to write on so they can share these with the class.

Whole class

Ask the class to comment on their improvements to the sentences by using the following words:
We improved these sentences by deleting .... and substituting ....for.....................This was the original sentence and this is the new one.
High attaining groups can share what they have done with the class.

Lesson 3

Whole class

Write up a sentence containing a subordinate clause. Revise children's knowledge of parts of sentences. Explain that you are all going to practise putting extra information into sentences by adding a subordinate clause, fitting it in between the pairs of commas. You will do this through playing Musical Clauses based on Copymaster 27. This game is an oral one, played with the class sitting in a circle.

Have ready in a bag a set of names of characters from books. Pupils start passing around the bag; play some music and when the music stops the child holding the bag selects a character card. He or she says the name and the next person must come up with a clause which gives some more information, then the next pupil finishes

it off. Start the music again and continue as in Pass the Parcel.

Small group and independent work

Using Copymaster 27, pupils in pairs either add in different clauses from the game or replace the characters' names with ones they prefer.

Differentiation

As the rest of the class.

Whole class

Pupils in pairs say their sentence without stating the character's name e.g. ...., *the laziest son in the world, threw the beans out of the window.* Pupils must a) guess the character's name then b) state the subordinate clause which has been added.

Lesson 4

Whole class

Play the same game but this time use the names of wild animals: *hawk, rat, snail, tarantula, python.*
Pupils add in a subordinate clause orally around the class.

Group and independent work

Pupils compose sentences individually using cards you

place on the table linked to subject areas across the curriculum.

Differentiation

As the rest of the class.

Whole class

Discuss why it is important to be able to write a sentence with a subordinate clause.
Collect the work, marking the use of commas to embed the subordinate clauses.

Lesson 5

Whole class

Use these two sentences from *The Angel of Nitshill Road* by Anne Fine to give an example of the use of the comma to aid meaning.
Read the following sentence aloud, first without the comma, then with the comma.
She stared at Celeste, then at the black book in her hand.
(Comma is used to make the reader pause and to make it clear that 'She' has seen two things – Celeste, and the black book. The choice of 'then' also aids meaning through emphasis.)
Say that the writer cannot actually speak to you where she could have used tone of voice to help meaning; the next best thing is punctuation to help meaning.
Say that reading aloud sentences to check on the appropriate use of punctuation, especially commas, helps to improve writing.
She's used up half the book already, writing down the horrid things he does. (The comma is used to make the reader pause before the subordinate clause, which gives an explanation of how she has used up half the book.)

Group and independent work

Use the first 4 sentences from Copymaster 26, section 3,

to enable pupils to think carefully about the use of the comma.
Ask them to read them aloud both with and without the comma, which will help them understand why the comma is being used.

Differentiation

Low Attainers – Work on the first sentence, where the comma is used to separate the information about when grandfather arrived and to emphasise it. Write a few more like this, cut them up, and ask pupils to put them together.
High Attainers – Work on the last two sentences and then write two more of their own, modelled on these.

Whole class

Ask the class to give you some reasons why commas are used in these sentences – write these under the sentences and put them up for the class to see.
Any of the sentences can be used as demonstration sentences for the class washing line if enlarged.
This work on sentences to be used as part of pupils' editing strategies. Check for a variety of sentence structure through the use of commas.

Theme 5) Fiction, film and print

Objectives

Text level
- 2 to investigate different versions of the same story in print or on film
- to identify similarities and differences; recognise how stories change over time; and identify differences of culture and place that are expressed in stories

Resources
Filmed versions of books and the original books.
Goodnight Mr Tom (BBC version) and *Goodnight Mr Tom* by Michelle Magorian.
Snow White in New York by Fiona French.
Little Inchkin by Fiona French.

Copymaster 28 – *Snow White* and *Snow White in New York*.
Copymaster 29 – *Goodnight Mr Tom* – film and book version.
Homework 15.

Assessment
At the end of this theme, is the pupil able to:
- investigate different versions of the same story in print or on film;
- identify similarities and differences;
- recognise how stories change over time;
- identify the differences of culture and place that are expressed in stories?

Lesson 1

Whole class

Explain that the next three lessons will be about comparing two books by Fiona French with the original fairy tales.
Summarise the story of *Snow White: Mother dies, father re-marries. New queen is jealous at Snow White's beauty. Arranges to have her killed. This fails. Snow White lost in the wood. Befriended by 7 dwarfs. Stepmother tries 3 times to kill her. Poisoned apple lodges in throat; Snow White unconscious, placed in coffin. Prince falls in love, has coffin carried to palace. Apple dislodges, Snow White comes to life, marries Prince.*

Now read *Snow White in New York*, pupils making notes in pairs (one pupil noting similarities, the other differences).

Independent and group activities
Using Copymaster 28 pupils note similarities and differences.

Differentiation
Low Attainers – Can have Copymaster 28 partially filled in.
High Attainers – Make notes on the style of the illustrations in comparison with the fairy tale, and how effective they are.

Whole class
Ask the class which they prefer, and why.

Lesson 2

Whole class

Tell the pupils that some fairy tales appear in many different countries, written in the language which is spoken in that country, with characters who dress and behave in the style or culture of the country.
Tell them that versions of *Cinderella* have been discovered in more than 100 different countries.
Say that the following story is based on *Tom Thumb*. Show them the cover of *Little Inchkin* and ask them to predict where this story is set (Japan).
Cover up the text and ask pupils to guess the story line from the illustrations alone.

Group and independent session
Using their notes alone, get pupils to draft out the complete story.

Differentiation
Low Attainers – Can have a scaffolded version to fill in.
High Attainers – Do the same task as the rest of the class.

Whole class
Read the actual story twice page by page. Ask pupils to evaluate how close their version was to the written one.

Lesson 3

Whole class

Now read a version of *Tom Thumb*.
Ask pupils to make notes of the key events.

Group and independent work
Using Copymaster 28 as a model, fill this in for *Tom Thumb* and *Little Inchkin*.

Differentiation
Low Attainers – Can have a partially filled in version.
High Attainers – Can comment on the effectiveness of the illustrations, making links with their comments on French's illustrations for *Snow White in New York*.

Whole class
Ask pupils to share with the class their completed comparisons and what they have learned from Fiona French's versions of fairy tales.

Lesson 4

Whole class

Tell the pupils that the next two lessons will be about comparing an extract from a book with how that extract has been filmed.
Read aloud the opening pages of *Goodnight Mr Tom*.

Group and independent work
Give out copies of the extract to pairs of pupils and ask them to prepare a storyboard as if they were film

directors, writing notes in each box for the cast to follow. Demonstrate this first.

Differentiation
Low Attainers – Have already read and discussed this extract and prepared the storyboard.
High Attainers – Add in background music to their notes.

Whole class
Different pairs explain their storyboards while the rest of the class make notes ready for tomorrow's lesson.

Lesson 5

Show the opening scenes of *Goodnight Mr Tom* and ask pupils to compare it with their storyboards.

Group and independent work
Give out Copymaster 29 and ask each pupil to fill it in, noting similarities and differences with the same extract they had yesterday.

Differentiation
All pupils work on the same task.

Whole class
Ask which version they prefer, and why, in order to reflect on learning.

Theme 6) Difference between author and narrator

Objectives

Text level
- 8 to distinguish between the author and the narrator, investigating narrative viewpoint and the treatment of different characters
- 9 to investigate the features of different fiction genres, discussing the appeal of popular fiction

Resources
Information sheets about a range of different authors from bookshops, catalogues and the Internet.
Collections of school or own books which pupils have read.

The Butterfly Lion – Michael Morpurgo; *The Story of Tracey Beaker* – Jacqueline Wilson; adventure books.
Copymaster 30 – A closer look at characters.
Copymaster 31 – *Jack and the Beanstalk* as it's never been told.
Homework 16.

Assessment
At the end of this theme, is the pupil able to:
- distinguish between author and narrator, and the use of the narrator in the story;
- use the remaining characters in a book to support and develop the story line?

Lesson 1

Whole class

Ask the class to give you a definition of an author and the names of up to 10 of their favourites. Ask if any pupils know anything about the authors they have written down.
Say that you will go into role as Roald Dahl (or any children's author you have researched) and they can interview you as an author (or you could ask a pupil to prepare this and be interviewed by the class).

Group and independent work
Give out information sheets on authors to each group and ask pupils, in pairs, to make brief notes.
One of each pair goes into role as the author and the other asks questions based on the notes.

Differentiation
Low Attainers – Pupils can be given ready prepared notes.
High Attainers – Pupils can use more than one piece of information from which to produce their notes.

Whole class
As author and interviewer, a number of pupils present their work from the independent session.
Ask the whole class to summarise what they have learnt about authors e.g. *different ages, sex, interests, backgrounds, old, young, attractive, plain, likes, dislikes* – no author falls into one category.
Ask pupils if they can say what the purpose of the lesson was in order to reflect on learning.

Lesson 2

Whole class

The Story of Tracey Beaker would be an excellent choice for this lesson. Show pupils the book's cover and ask who wrote it – Jacqueline Wilson (the author). If she was one of the authors studied in yesterday's lesson, ask pupils what they know about her.
Read out the first two pages and ask who is telling it – Tracey Beaker. Read the blurb from the back of the book because it includes Tracey talking about herself in the first person and a description of her situation in the third person.
Introduce the word **narrator** – say that Tracey Beaker is the narrator of this story. Pupils will more used to describing her as one of the characters in the book – the main character. You could demonstrate changing some sentences from 1st to 3rd person to show the difference between the character as narrator and the author as narrator.

Now ask them what the difference is between author and narrator.

Group and independent work
Give each group a selection of books they have already read and ask them to read the opening pages and name the narrator(s); as they are familiar with the story, ask each pupil to write no more than 50 words describing the narrator (if there are several, ask them to choose one).

Differentiation
Low Attainers – Draw a quick sketch of the narrator with labels.
High Attainers – Choose a narrator from two books by the same author. Are the narrators similar characters?

Whole class
Ask all pupils why authors use a narrator (to tell their stories from a certain point of view). Ask for a few examples and the views of the narrator.

Lesson 3

Whole class

Show pupils Copymaster 30 and demonstrate how to fill one in.
Then ask pupils to fill it in using the book they chose yesterday. This is likely to take a large part of the lesson.

Differentiation

Low Attainers – Identify the narrator and one other character.
High Attainers – Draw arrows across the chart and make links between characters: when they meet, their relationship etc.

Whole class

Ask what they have learned about why characters and a narrator are needed in a book.

Lesson 4

Whole class

Use Michael Morpurgo's book *The Butterfly Lion*.
It is important that pupils have either all read the book or that you have read it to them.
The author has used more than one narrator to tell the story.
Read out an extract from each narrator: the boy at the beginning and end of the story, Bertie, the old lady.
Ask why the author needs to do this (because the story moves through time and different settings).

Group and independent work

Give out a selection of the extracts you used and ask each pupil to write why each narrator was important for each section of the story, with a 50-word description of each narrator.

Differentiation

Low Attainers – Work on one section of the story, which they have been helped with.
High Attainers – Ask them to write about what would happen to the story if one of the characters were left out.

Whole class

Ask pupils to summarise the role of the narrator.

Lesson 5

Whole class

Remind them that *The Butterfly Lion* used different narrators to tell the story.
Say that some stories are written so that the same story is told by different narrators, so that we can appreciate that there can be more than one side to a story.
Say that you are going to plan one of these versions together.
Use Copymaster 31 as a planner and demonstrate how to fill in one section. Use the following notes if you wish on Jack's views/feelings:
• *Fed up with my mother scolding me*
• *Going up the Beanstalk was better than staying at home*
• *Amazed by the giant's golden goose*
• *Decided the giant would not miss the goose*
• *Escaped just in time*
• *Pleased with golden goose.*

Group and independent work

Ask each pupil to plan the remaining sections.

Differentiation

Low Attainers – Give a cloze text.
High Attainers – Ask them to write a section of the story from the giant's wife's point of view.

Whole class

Ask a selection of pupils to use their plan for an oral telling by the narrator or character. Ask what the narrators in this story have to offer the reader.

Theme 7 Myths, legends and fables

Objectives

Text level

- 1 to identify and classify the features of myths, legends and fables
- 11 to write own versions of myths, legends and fables, using structures and themes identified in reading
- 13 to review and edit writing to produce a final form, matched to the needs of an identified reader

Sentence level

- 3 to understand how writing can be adapted to different audiences and purposes
- 10 to ensure that, in using pronouns, it is clear to what or to whom they refer

Resources

Any collections of myths, fables and legends.
A definition of a myth, legend and fable, written on card, for the wall or washing line.
A copy of *Narcissus* from 'Myths and Legends' ed. A. Horowitz (Kingfisher).
Copymasters 32 and 33. Homework 17.

Assessment

At the end of this theme, is the pupil able to:

- distinguish between myths, fables and legends by reading and analysing a number of texts;
- produce a final form based on one of these, paying attention to the use of pronouns and applying proof-reading and editing techniques?

Lesson 1

Whole class

Explain to the pupils that in this unit they will be looking at myths, legends and fables.
Put up the definition of each: **Myth** – *an ancient story of gods or heroes which addresses a problem or concern which humans experience, e.g. jealousy, love, hatred;* **Legend** – *a traditional story about heroes such as King Arthur, which may be based on truth, but which has 'grown' over the years;* **Fable** – *a short story written to teach a moral lesson.* Show the class some of the resources and give an example of each text type with a brief summary of the story line. Demonstrate how to fill in Copymaster 32 using some of the pupils' own suggestions from those they have read or heard themselves. Add some of your own if pupils cannot contribute many, e.g. *The Boy who Cried*

Wolf (fable), *Odysseus and the Cyclops* (myth), *Tales of King Arthur* (legend).

Group and independent work

Hand out selections of books or copies of stories and ask pupils to read one in turn, the whole group participating in the reading. Ask the group to discuss which category it falls into, using Copymaster 32.

Differentiation

Low Attainers – Ensure that the stories are within their reading ability range.
High Attainers – Can add some more questions to Copymaster 32.

Whole class

Ask one pupil from each group to share Copymaster 32 with the rest of the class.

Lesson 2

Whole class

Show a filled in Copymaster 32 for *The Travellers and the Bear* by Aesop, or choose a different one.
Read the fable then plan a modern version of the same fable but written for 7 year olds in simple English. Demonstrate how to start one off: Jo and Tom were travelling together through the safari park when their car broke down. They both got out of the car, then they saw a lion approaching. Without thinking of Tom, Jo climbed up a lamp-post nearby . . .

Group and independent work

In pairs pupils work to produce a simple version of no more than a paragraph.

Differentiation

Low Attainers – Can be given some ready-made ideas *e.g. two friends having a picnic. An angry bull charges at them.*
High Attainers – Can transform this into a cartoon with fantastic characters *e.g. Superman.*

Whole class

Ask several pairs to explain the changes they made, how they matched them to the age and the underlying purpose of the writing.

Lesson 3

Whole class

Tell the class that the theme is vanity and ask them to define this.

Read the whole story of *Narcissus*.

Say that the task is for them to write a modernised version of the same story by using Copymaster 33.

Make links with yesterday's activity on the fable.

Say that this time the reader is a person of their own age and the purpose of the writing is to show the mistake of a person who loves himself/herself above everything else.

Independent work

Every pupil works on the same plan, then starts a first draft of their story.

Whole class

Various pupils share their plans, stating the differences between the ancient and modern versions.

Lesson 4

Whole class

Choose someone's plan then begin by demonstrating a few sentences, e.g. *Lee put the finishing touches to his make-up and then paused to admire himself. "What a hunk!" he chuckled to himself...*

Use the whole session for the finishing of the stories, which then must be proofread and edited.

Ask each pupil to check that pronouns are correct, especially if the sex of the main character has changed, as this will need careful attention to the correct choice of he/she, him/her.

Collect the books in at this stage and mark for audience and purpose and efficient proof-reading and editing.

Lesson 5

Whole class

Each pupil produces a finished, polished modern-day version of *Narcissus* during this final session. These are all to be placed in a Big Book whose front cover shows pictures of fashionable models, film stars and pop stars. This could have the title Narcissus found alive and well in the year 2001.

Theme 8) Non-chronological reports

Objectives

Text level
- 16 to prepare for reading by identifying what they already know and what they need to find out
- 17 to locate information confidently and efficiently through (i) using contents, indexes, sections, headings (ii) skimming to gain overall sense of text (iii) scanning to locate specific information (iv) close reading to aid understanding (v) text-marking (vi) using CD Rom and other sources, where available
- 22 to plan, compose edit and refine short non-chronological reports, using reading as a source, focusing on clarity, conciseness and impersonal style

Resources
Books, encyclopaedias, magazines, CD Roms as sources of information linked to other curriculum areas.

A set of cards which have the key features of reports written on them.
A collection of bird books/CD Rom.
Copymaster 34. Homework 18.

Assessment
At the end of this theme, is the pupil able to:
- identify what he/she already knows about a subject and what he/she needs to find out;
- use information books confidently and efficiently, locating what he/she needs through skimming and scanning reading techniques;
- use his/her notes as the basis for short non-chronological reports;
- analyse and discuss the text features of such reports?

Lesson 1

Explain to the class that this week they are to join The Fact-Finding Expedition!
Remind them of their work on research skills:
- Write down what you already know about a subject
- Sort it out
- Decide which aspects you need to research
- Locate the resources you need
- Use them efficiently to get answers to your questions.

The following words could be displayed on a washing line or on A4 sheets which have been laminated:
indexes, contents, sections, headings, pictures, diagrams, charts, skimming, scanning, close reading, text marking (if appropriate).
Write up the word *starlings* and ask pupils to tell you anything they know; quickly write this down in a bullet point list on a large sheet of paper (keep it for tomorrow) and then ask them to group the facts in some way. Underline facts which go together in the same colour: *appearance, habitat, diet, breeding* etc.

Group and independent work
Divide the class into groups and ask each group to come up with questions they would like answered, linked to one of these headings.
Using the books on the table or the computer, ask pupils in pairs to find answers to their questions. Write the questions on post-it notes (keep these).
Write their answers on post-it notes (keep these).

Differentiation
Low Attainers – Given simpler texts.
High Attainers – As the rest of the class.

Whole class
Run through the research techniques one by one, asking pupils to say how useful each was to find their answers.

Lesson 2

Write up these headings: *appearance, habitat, diet, breeding.*
Refer to the list from yesterday and add in the facts pupils already knew.
Collect their post-it question notes from yesterday and stick them on the board. Peel them off one by one and ask for the answer: add this to the correct heading.
Incorporate these in a report which you write in front of them – you may like to incorporate ideas from the text below. Talk aloud as you do, using the correct terms as below.
Starlings are familiar, noisy, bustling birds.
Classification – *What they are.* They live in large groups and nest in towns or the countryside.
Description – *Where they live.* In winter, starlings have black feathers covered in small cream spots. In summer they are mostly unspotted. They are 21 cm long. *What they look like.* They eat insects, worms, spiders, slugs and various fruits. *What they eat.* 5 to 7 eggs hatch after 12 to 13 days and the young leave the nest 20 to 22 days later. *Breeding habits.* Most people like starlings as they are good mimics. **Comment**. If the flocks are very large – some flocks number hundreds of thousands – they are not as popular because of the mess and noise that they make. **Summary**.

Group and independent work
Give each group a selection of facts about sparrows – Copymaster 34. Ask them to organise them and write a report on sparrows in the style of the one on starlings.

Differentiation
Low Attainers – Can be given Copymaster 34 and decide where the missing parts are.
High Attainers – Will be expected to have detailed, accurate texts.

Whole class
Ask the whole class to swap their work with a partner and mark it against the key features.

Lessons 3 and 4

Whole class

Explain to pupils that now each of them will research facts in pairs for a report linked to a different subject area. (It is useful to do this unit at the beginning of a new topic area in science, history or geography.)
Start by asking them to jot down anything at all they know about this subject area – *e.g. comparisons between London and Tokyo as a geography topic.*
Write a bullet point list and then ask them to sort the list into key headings: *local features (rivers, roads); population; industries; language; food.*
Say that they can keep these headings and use them as subheadings for their finished text.

Group and independent work

Divide pupils into groups of researchers and ask them to write down questions they need answers for.
Copy several sheets of information on London and Tokyo for each group, and ask them to mark with a highlighter pen the sections which will be useful then make notes as covered in Autumn Term, Theme 3.

Differentiation

Low Attainers – May need support on skimming and scanning reading techniques. Work on this with them as part of guided reading.
High Attainers – Will be expected to find answers to their questions from a much broader range of books.

Research will be spread across the remaining part of the hour and for the whole of tomorrow's lesson.

Lesson 5

Whole class

Pupils will by now have assembled their facts.

Remind them to use subheadings in their reports and to work towards presenting them in the finished form.
Collect these in and mark for clarity, conciseness and impersonal style.

Theme 9) Information sources

Objectives

Text level
- 18 to understand how authors record and acknowledge their sources
- 19 to evaluate texts critically by comparing how different sources treat the same information
- 23 to record and acknowledge sources in their own writing

Resources
A selection of information books on the same topics, including CD Roms. These may be the same collection of books from the theme before this one. Other information books that contain photographs and pictures e.g. 'The Water Cycle' (Wayland), 'Deserts' (Two-can).

Dictionaries that include photographs e.g. 'Collins Junior Dictionary'; 'Collins Primary Dictionary'. Encyclopaedias e.g. OUP set of encyclopaedias. A selection of photographs drawn from other curriculum areas, some accompanied by written text.
A selection of real photographs with text to match. Number fans.
Small pieces of card for covering up the text
Copymasters 35 and 36. Homework 19.

Assessment
At the end of this theme, is the pupil able to:
- evaluate which books he/she finds the most useful;
- know where authors usually acknowledge their sources, and why they need to do this?

Lesson 1

Whole Class

Explain to the class that they are going to be critics. Say that professional critics read books and then write reviews to go in newspapers. People who buy newspapers often read the reviews before they buy a book. Ask if they read reviews of films before they decide which film to see in the cinema or borrow from the video shop.
Explain that today they will look critically at the use of photographs as an information source Display a page from a Non-Fiction Big Book, which has text and a large photograph. Ask the class to read the text aloud. Write up the questions below and then get the class to look at the photo with a critical eye, using the list of questions to help with their opinions:

- Subject matter obvious?   • Sharp image?   • Does it catch the eye?   • Does it help explain the text?

Give the class 1 minute in pairs to discuss it, then ask for feedback.

Turn to the page which displays a heading such as 'Acknowledgements/Photographic credits/Picture acknowledgements, and explain that authors must write down/acknowledge the name of the photographer or/and the book it came from in the first place, as part of copyright laws.

Group and independent work
In small groups, pairs of pupils choose an information book from a pile on the table and work to evaluate up to 5 photographs; ask them to write the title & publisher and locate the source of the photo, then fill in a table like the one below:
Differentiation by outcome

Whole Class
Pupils choose the best photograph they looked at and evaluate it orally, using their filled in tables as a guide.

The Water Cycle – Wayland — Page 25	Water in a stream – P. Brown
Subject matter obvious?	Yes
Sharp image	Yes
Does it catch the eye?	Yes
Does it help explain the text?	Yes

Lesson 2

Whole Class

Explain that today they will look critically at the use of pictures drawn by an artist as an information source. Display a page from a Non-Fiction Big Book, which has text and a large picture. Ask the class to read the text aloud. Write up the following questions and then get the class to look at the picture with a critical eye, using the questions to help with their opinions:

- Subject matter obvious?   • Colours and style are suitable   • Does it catch the eye?   • Does it help explain the text?

Give the class 1 minute in pairs to discuss it, then ask for feedback.
Turn to the acknowledgements page and find out who is the illustrator. Explain that authors must write down/acknowledge the name of the illustrator or/and the book it came from in the first place, as part of copyright laws.

Group and independent work
In small groups, pairs of pupils choose an information book from a pile on the table and work to evaluate at least 2 photographs and two pictures; ask them to write the title & publisher and locate the source of the photo and the artwork, then fill in a table like the one below.

Differentiation by outcome

Whole Class

Ask pupils to express their views on why authors usually use a mix of photo's and artwork in information books.

Title and publisher:	Description of photo/picture:
Subject matter obvious?	
Sharp image	
Does it catch the eye?	
Does it help explain the text?	

Lesson 3

Display a large version of Copymaster 35 and the photo and text from lesson 1.

Say that the aim of the lesson is to see if the text actually **refers** to the photo **and** helps the reader to understand the information.

Ask the class to read the text silently and jot down the words in the text which refer to the picture.

Then hold up a number fan, selecting a rating for the effectiveness of the text in conveying information to the reader

Discuss what they come up with – say they are reading the photo and the text as a real critic would!

Group and independent work

In pairs, ask pupils to transfer the information about either a photo or a picture. from their previous days' work, on to Copymaster 35.

Then to fill in the rest of the copymaster as you modelled it at the start of the lesson.

Differentiation

Low Attainers – Place a teaching assistant with the lowest ability group who will help pupils focus on the key words in the text which refer to their photo, or pre-select the words and write them on cards and ask the pupils to find them in the text.

High Attainers – Ask them to read the text carefully and make one suggestion how it might be improved e.g. shorter sentences, different word choices…

Whole Class

Ask pupils to say what they learned from this activity about the job of a critic.

Lesson 4

Whole Class

Show the class two books on the same theme e.g. pets

Turn to the index and find the same word e.g. sleep

Turn to this section in each of the books in turn and discuss with the children how each author has written it in a different way, with different artwork.

Model how to fill in Copymaster 35 for each of the books.

Group and independent work

In groups, ask pairs of pupils to choose two different information books on the same theme from the pile on their tables.

Ask pupils to skim the contents pages of both books and to find a similar aspect of the theme of the book e.g. 'diet' from a book on pets; choose a page with a photo or art work and evaluate it using Copymaster 35.

Differentiation

Low Attainers – Read and study simple texts

High Attainers – Jot down a text explanation which they have written if the one in the book is not clear enough.

Whole Class

Ask pairs of pupils to express a preference for one of the books, using their copymaster as the basis for the explanation

Lesson 5

Using the big non-fiction information book you used yesterday, look at other features: cover, synopsis, contents introduction, chapter headings, sub headings, lay out, type of font, mix of photos, pictures, diagrams, charts, page numbers on all the pages, index, other features. Demonstrate how to fill in Copymaster 35.

Group and independent work

Each pair should return to the books they used yesterday and fill in the evaluation sheet Copymaster 35.

Differentiation - the same for the whole class

Whole Class

Ask the whole class to give the rating for their books, saying why some books had higher /lower ratings.

Theme 10) Poetry anthologies

Objectives

Text level
• 7 to compile a class anthology of favourite poems with commentaries which illuminate the choices
• 12 to use the structure of poems read to write extensions based on these

Resources
Copymaster 37 – Spinning their magic: a commentary web.

Copymaster 38 – *The Way through the Woods* by Rudyard Kipling.
Poetry anthologies.
Homework 20.

Assessment
At the end of this theme, is the pupil able to:
• select comments for a critical commentary of a poem they enjoy;
• produce an extension of a poem?

Lesson 1

Whole class

Say that the purpose of the unit is: to choose a selection of narrative poems pupils really like for a class anthology; to explain why they like them and to share these in school and with a wider audience via the Internet; to use some of these poems as the model for writing some of their own.
Give out an example of Copymaster 37 to every pupil and explain and demonstrate how to fill one in, using, for example, *The Listeners* from earlier in the term.

Group and independent work
Using two narrative poems from earlier this term, ask each pupil to choose a poem and fill in Copymaster 37.

(You could include the rap based on *The Highwayman*.)

Differentiation
Low Attainers – Are given one poem and then go on to fill in Copymaster 37 in pairs.
High Attainers – Add two statements of their own into the web to give a more 'expanded' commentary.

Whole class
Ask 5 pupils to use their Copymasters as favourable commentaries on the poems, justifying why they would include these in a class anthology.

Lessons 2 and 3

Group work

Move straight into group work by handing out copies of up to five new poems to each group over the course of two days.
In pairs this time, ask pupils to skim through all the poems and then fill in a Copymaster for each one.

Differentiation
Low Attainers – Have help with reading and talking about the poems before they fill in the Copymasters.

High Attainers – Continue to work on more detailed commentaries to illuminate their choices.

Whole class
During Lesson 3, when enough poems have been commented upon, write up the title of each of the poems in turn and ask for a selection of commentaries. Make final decisions on 5 poems for the anthology, and include a selection from Copymaster 37 in the anthology.

Lesson 4

Whole class

Using a large or OHT version of *The Way through the Woods* by Rudyard Kipling, first read and ask for comments if you have not already used it in the previous week.

Explain that you are going to model how to extend the poem. You will keep the same rhyme pattern but change some of the content. The main change will be through changing the season.

Model how to plan the extension. You may wish to use the chart below to help you. Demonstrate how to turn the plan into a verse, e.g.

They shut the road through the woods, eighty years ago, Frost and snow have undone it again . . . That, where the barn owl broods.

Group and independent work

Give the groups an empty version of the chart for Spring and Autumn, plus a copy of the poem.

In pairs, they choose a season and write a new version of this verse.

Differentiation

Low Attainers – Have a table for Spring or Autumn, already filled in.

Now ask them to make changes to the first verse. The verse could be ready on disk and pupils need only highlight and replace certain words, resulting in an easier task all round.

High Attainers – Write out one verse and then use the same table to make decisions on what they could change in the second verse, matching the season they have used in the first verse.

Whole class

Ask pupils from each group to run through the changes they made, without stating the season. Ask the class to guess which season it is.

Collect the verses in and select two good examples of an Autumn and a Spring verse.

The Way Through the Woods	My extension
Season: Summer	Season: Winter
Weather: wet	Weather: cold
Birds: ring-doves	Birds: owls
Time: 70 years ago	Time: 80 years ago

Lesson 5

Whole class

Copy all four verses: the original verse, your Winter model demonstrated at the beginning of lesson 4, one Spring example and one Autumn example.

Take the original verse and sketch the scene quickly in front of the class, drawing arrows to a small text box and writing which materials/colours/textures/software you will use when completing an illustration for this verse. Only write two text boxes.

Group and independent work

Give 4 groups a different verse each then, independently, ask pupils to follow your model of a quick sketch followed by text boxes, in preparation for their illustration.

Differentiation

Low Attainers – Can complete the example you have already started on.

High Attainers – Can complete this task then prepare some questions to ask you, writing different questions on cards.

Whole class

The high attaining group distribute their questions amongst the class and then you answer.

This work support Art and Design at KS2. When the illustrations are worked upon during an Art and Design lesson, allow pupils to mount and display their illustrations on a wall, grouped into seasons. If this poem has been chosen for the class anthology, some of these illustrations could be added to it.

Theme 1 Writing from different cultures

Objectives

Text level

- 1 to investigate a range of texts from different cultures, considering patterns of relationships, social customs, attitudes and beliefs:
  - identify these features by reference to the text
  - consider and evaluate these features in relation to their own experience
- 10 to write discursively about a novel or story, *e.g. to describe, explain or comment on it*

Resources

Little House on the Prairie – Laura Ingalls Wilder; (*Ali and the Came* – dual language text) Arabic/English – Fay Gabriel; *The Gift of the Sun – A Tale from South Africa –* Dianne Stewart; *Journey to Jo'burg* – Beverley Naidoo; Information books/CD ROM on Tobago; *Gregory Cool* by Caroline Binch.
Whiteboards and markers.
Copymaster 39. Homework 21.

Assessment

At the end of this theme is the pupil able to:

- investigate a range of texts from different cultures, exploring social customs, attitudes and beliefs;
- identify these features through reference to the text;
- consider and evaluate these features and relate them to his/her own experience;
- write explanations, descriptions or comments about a novel or story?

Lesson 1

Whole class

Enlarge an extract from *The Little House on the Prairie* Chapter 9 beginning with 'That afternoon Ma sat sewing in the shade of the house' to the scene where she places the china woman on the mantleshelf.
Tell pupils to jot down anything they notice about the country, family or way of life.
Get them to share their observations with you. Then ask them to relate the episode in the story to their own lives if they can – moving to a new country, settling in.

Group and independent work

Give out some more extracts from the same book and ask them to jot down anything more they notice under the headings: *country, family, way of life*, using quotes from the text.

Differentiation

Low Attainers – Could be helped with the extracts either beforehand or during the task; use reading scheme books set in different cultures.
High Attainers – Write a list of what they think the parents' attitudes are to this new country and prepare to be interviewed by the class.

Whole class

The whole class asks questions of one group of pupils who are in role as the parents.

Lesson 2

Whole class

Today, give out copies of *Mma*, a chapter from *Journey to Jo'burg*.
Ask the children to use the same headings as yesterday and jot note what they work out from the text including some quotes to justify their point of view.

Group and independent work

This is to be completed in the following 20 minutes as a group reading task.
Say that their notes will need to be used for the role-play which will follow.

Differentiation

Low Attainers – Given an easier book *e.g. Gift of the Sun* or *Ali's Camel*.
High Attainers – Make comparisons between yesterday's text and today's.

Whole class

Hand out character cards: Tiro, Naledi, Mma, the white lady, Grace. Group the class into a circle.
Ask questions based on country, family relationships and way of life, with pupils answering in role. Ask if they can relate the episode in the book to their own lives.

Lessons 3 and 4

Whole class

This work will take two days.

Explain to the class that they are going to research information on Tobago, which will be needed when they discuss as a class a book set in Tobago during Lesson 5. Ask what they already know and make a list, then ask them to sort the list into these headings: *food, occupations of the people, description of the island, wildlife.*

Small group and independent work

Each group makes notes for their heading, and prepares a bullet point list to share with the class – on large sheets of paper.

Differentiation

Low Attainers – Are given a ready prepared mix of information on Tobago and sort this out under the appropriate headings, and then use simple information books to find some more facts.

High Attainers – Are given Tobagan recipes and asked to work out typical ingredients easily available on the island, then find more information about each one – appearance, sweet or savoury, how to prepare it for cooking.

Whole class

Taking each heading in turn, read out their lists, and then choose several pupils to interview you (in role as a visitor to the island) where you talk about things you have enjoyed in Tobago which are different from those in England, including customs.

Lesson 5

Whole class

Read aloud the whole of *Gregory Cool*, then ask them to relate any factual information in the story to their own research.

Independent work

Every pupil to fill in Copymaster 39 and then draft two paragraphs of no more than 50 words each about Gregory's negative and positive experiences on the island, referring to customs they have noted.

Whole class

Collect work in and mark for pupils writing clearly about family relationships, attitudes and customs.

Theme 2) Points of view

Objectives

- 2 to identify the point of view from which a story is told and how this affects the reader's response
- 3 to change point of view, *e.g. describe a situation from the point of view of another character or perspective*
- 7 to write from another character's point of view *e.g. re-telling an incident in letter form*
- 9 to write in the style of the author.

Resources

The Story of Tracey Beaker; The Suitcase Kid; The Lottie Project – all by Jacqueline Wilson. *The Stone Menagerie* by Anne Fine.
The Midnight Fox – Betsy Byars; *Danny, the Champion of the World* – Roald Dahl; *The Hodgeheg* – Dick King-Smith; *Harry Potter and The Philosopher's Stone* – J.K. Rowling.

Just Ferret – Gene Kemp; *The Highwayman; A Stack of Storypoems* – Tony Bradman.
Packs of group reading books which have been read very recently.
Whiteboards and pens.
Copymaster 40. Homework 22.

Assessment

At the end of this theme is the pupil able to:
- know quite clearly how 'points of view' can be expressed in writing and use this effectively in his/her own writing;
- demonstrate an improvement in his/her editing and proof-reading skills in pieces of writing which are to be published?

Lesson 1

Whole class

Enter into this unit through **role-play**.
Either do it yourself or rehearse pupils who are willing and confident. Suggested extracts: Chapter 2 of *Harry Potter and the Philosopher's Stone* – in role as Aunt Potter telling Harry to get up; Chapter entitled *E is for Ethel* of *The Suitcase Kid*, in role as Andy, from 'For most of my life' up to 'another baby'; Opening paragraph from *The Hodgeheg*. After each question and answer session to the person in role, fill in the table below:

Group and independent work

Hand out extracts from *The Lottie Project* by Jacqueline Wilson and ask pupils to jot down the point of view of the named character and what the author is trying to make the reader feel, as in the table below.

Differentiation

Low Attainers – Read the Lottie extract – School pp 17-18 and discuss their views about Lottie. Ask them to write two questions for someone in the group who will role-play Lottie and to rehearse the answers to reveal clearly how she is feeling.
Average and High Attainers – Read the extract where Charlotte shows her feelings towards Jamie pp 12-13. Ask them to write two questions for someone in the group who will role-play Charlotte and to rehearse the answers to reveal clearly how she is feeling.

Whole Class

Two groups present their role-play to the class. As a result of this, the class suggests how to fill in the missing sections in the table below.

Book Title & author	'Point of view of character'	What the author is trying to make the reader feel
Harry Potter and the Philosopher's Stone J.K.Rowling	Aunt Petunia resents Harry	Pity for Harry, anger towards Aunt Petunia
The Suitcase Kid Jacqueline Wilson	Andy resents the changes in her life because of the divorce	How angry and hurt a child can feel when parents have split up
The Hodgeheg Dick-King Smith	Ma is very worried about the dangers of busy traffic	Sympathy with Ma because of the dangerous traffic
The Lottie Project Jacqueline Wilson	Charlotte feels……..	
The Lottie Project Jacqueline Wilson	Lottie feels………….	

Lesson 2

Whole class

The objective of this lesson will be to write a diary entry from another character's point of view which has not been expressed in the book.

Model how to write the opening lines of a diary entry for Miss Beckworth. Expect pupils to write in the rest of what she may have written, but also model the beginning of the last sentence in the dairy entry. when she expresses her real views about Charlotte.

First Day of Term

Met an interesting new girl today: Charlotte Enright. She was quite a challenge. First she insisted her name was Charlie. Then she.....

However, underneath I think she is.......

Group and independent work

In pairs, give pupils time to complete the missing parts of the diary entry.

Differentiation

Low Attainers – Are given a 'cloze' diary text, where they fill in missing words.

High Attainers – Write a diary entry for Jamie, using the same style as in the teacher's model

Whole Class

Ask several pairs of pupils to read out their completed diary entries. Ask the class to explain how a diary entry like this in the book might have changed their views about Miss Beckworth and Charlotte.

Lesson 3

Whole Class

Put up a large version of Copymaster 40 and explain that they are going to explore viewpoints of other characters in *The Lottie Project*.

Read out the following pages from the chapter called 'Home' – from the beginning of the chapter on page 19 to 'We were saving' at the top of page 22.

Model how to fill in the chart for the first four boxes. Leave the bottom box blank and the 4 speech bubbles.

Group and independent work

Explain that the children now have to choose one of the following characters and write the missing text on their personal whiteboards: Grandma, Grandpa, Jo (Charlotte's mother).

Then fill in one of the speech bubbles with something the character may have said.

All pupils work at the same task.

Whole Class

Ask the class to sit in a circle and choose up to 10 pupils to say aloud their speech bubbles. After each pupil has spoken, the class can ask one question to establish their point of view.

The viewpoint of another character who sees /witnesses this event (write it in the first person or third person)

Lessons 4 and 5

Tell the class that they are all going to write in a scene into *The Lottie Project* which will be the row that took place between Grandpa, Grandma and Jo when Jo told them that she and Charlotte were moving to live on the run-down Newborough Estate.

They are doing this in order to help the readers of this book sympathise with Grandma and Grandpa's point of view.

Model how to do this as follows: -

Give the scene a title: The Row

Write an example of a possible beginning to the row as follows – keep talking about the text as you are writing, about the content and punctuation needed. Talk to the children about how the choices of verbs (as underlined) should be angry, aggressive ones for Mum and pitiful, quieter ones for Grandma and Grandpa, in order to get the reader to sympathise with the grandparents. Also how the bold font can sway a reader by showing a louder voice.

The Row

' I cannot believe what you have just told us,' Grandma <u>whispered.</u>

' Well, it's the **truth**!' <u>yelled</u> Mum. 'We are not going to live **here** any more.'

'After all we have done for you!' <u>said</u> Grandma, beginning to cry.

'It's time to go and it will be the **best** thing for us,' <u>shouted</u> Mum, her face becoming flushed.

Group and independent work

Expect that the class will continue this work in silence, individually, re-reading as they go along to make sure that they have the right emphasis of angry Jo and poor, put-upon grandparents.

Differentiation – by outcome, the teacher sitting with groups and advising children. at the point of writing, on how they are meeting the requirements of the task.

When individual children have finished the writing, they must re-read it again as a proof reader, checking on spelling and punctuation.

Then the pupils will sit tighter in pairs as response partners to each other's work.

When this has been responded to, they can write a final version to go in a class Big Book entitled: **The Lottie Project – Changing Readers' Views**

Theme 3 Poetry

Objectives

Text level

- 4 to read, rehearse and modify performance of poetry
- 5 to select poetry and justify their choices *e.g. in compiling their class anthology*
- 11 to use performance poems as models to write and to produce poetry in polished forms through revising, redrafting and presentation

Word level

- 11 to use a range of dictionaries and understand their purposes *e.g. idioms.*

Resources

Tom's Guinea Pig by Gwen Dunn from *A Stack of Story Poems*; *The Weather* by Gavin Ewart; *Mango* by Grace Nichols; *Give up Slimming, Mum* by Kit Wright all from *Footprints on the Page* or any other poems you enjoy hearing read aloud.
Copymaster 41 – Performance poetry.
Copymaster 42 – *The Weather* by Gavin Ewart.
Homework 23.

Assessment

At the end of this theme is the pupil able to:

- select a poem which he/she understands will be interesting or entertaining and present it to an audience;
- be aware of the importance of voice, gesture and eye contact when performing poetry;
- write a performance poem of his/her own based on a model selected by the teacher?

Lessons 1 and 2

Whole class

Explain to the class that you have selected some poems which you think are good for reading aloud, and that this week they will be reading, performing and writing poems, as well as selecting poems for their class anthology.

Read aloud two poems, using your voice well to create interest and aid meaning, using gesture and eye contact to 'catch' your audience. As you read, ask pupils to think about why you chose these poems – and how you read them aloud or performed them. (They are funny and catch your interest; they rhyme and are easy to read; they do not rhyme but you can read them in interesting ways; they are about things which people are interested in; use of voice, eye contact and gesture.)

Show a large version of Copymaster 41 and divide the class into half.

Ask one group to say what they liked about the content of the poem and the other group to comment on how you read or performed it.

Give pupils one minute to discuss this, then fill in Copymaster 41 using their comments.

Group and independent work

The rest of today and tomorrow's lesson will be spent on pairs of pupils completing the following tasks:

A Selecting a poem for performance from a selection of poetry books
B Filling in Copymaster 41
C Rehearsing the poem
D Copying/word processing the poem for the class anthology.

Differentiation

Low Attainers – Choose easier to read poems but still use Copymaster 41.
High Attainers – Complete the same task as the rest of the class.

Lesson 3

Group work

In pairs, ask one pupil to perform the poem and the other pupil to say why it was chosen and the effects they wanted to have on the audience through the way they performed it. They may refer to their completed Copymaster 41 if they need to.

Lessons 4 and 5

Whole class

Use Copymaster 42 as an OHT or enlarge it.
Perform the poem with some passion!
Remind them of what metaphors are and how the
weather is being written about as if it is human.
Tell the pupils that this poem will be the model they will
all use as the basis for writing a new performance poem.
They will plan, draft and edit their poems, then prepare
their new poems for performance during the last lesson.

Group and independent work

Tell them to keep the first and last lines, but then work
to the following plan:

1 Make a list of nouns connected with the weather:
*sleet, mist, thunder, lightning, gale, hurricane, storm, fog,
cloud . . .*

2 Study each line in turn and replace the subject in each
sentence (*rain, sun, hail, snow, wind, mud and ice*) with a
different subject (noun) from their new list
3 Now think about how to complete the sentence,
trying out different ways.
Model one line *e.g. Why is the sleet so mean to us?*

Differentiation

Low Attainers – Keep the same subject (noun) in each
question but add a different ending.
High Attainers – Try out some metaphors the same way
as the author did, to make the noun do something
humans can do – *glare, dance, be fond of*, upset us – or
be – *a tearaway, an overall*.

Whole class

Pupils are selected to read out their poems, saying what
it is that they changed and how easy/difficult this was.

Theme 4) Letters

This unit should be linked to other curriculum areas where a letter is sent to a real audience.

Objectives

Text level
- 12 to read and evaluate letters *e.g. from newspapers, magazines* intended to inform, protest, complain, persuade, considering:
  - (i) how they are set out
  - (ii) how language is used *e.g. to gain attention, respect, manipulate*
- 17 to draft and write individual, group or class letters for real purposes *e.g. put a point of view, comment, protest*; to edit and present to a finished state

Resources
Letters from local and national newspapers to inform, protest, complain and persuade.
Four captions: to inform, to protest, to complain, to persuade,
Copymasters 43, 44, 45, 46 and 47. Homework 24.

Assessment
At the end of this theme is the pupil able to:
- read and work out four different purposes for letters – to inform, protest, complain and persuade;
- analyse key features which are present in letters like these and use the ones they have read as models to plan, draft and produce a final version of a letter which is sent off to a real audience?

Lesson 1

Whole class

Explain to the class that the theme is aimed at helping them understand the different purposes and styles of letters found in newspapers and magazines.
Say that you are about to read out two letters.
Their underlying purpose – why they have been written – will match two of the four captions you now display: to inform, to protest, to complain, to persuade.
Enlarge two of these letters or put them on an OHT.
Read them to the class and give pupils one minute to decide on the purpose of both letters.

Group and independent work
Give out both copies of these letters and the following task:
Letter A (Copymaster 43) What is the information? To whom was it sent? Why was it sent? Underlying purpose? Does the writer expect a reply?

Letter B (Copymaster 44) What is the writer protesting about? What are the reasons for the protest? Will any action be taken? What feelings are coming over to the reader? Does the writer expect a reply? Underlying purpose?
Use different colour pens to underline the different parts of each letter to match the question. One group to have copies on OHT, marking the sections with OHP pens.

Differentiation
Low Attainers – Put in labelled boxes to show the organisation of the letter, matching the questions above.
High Attainers – Look in more detail at the kind of language used in the letters *e.g. fairly pleasant, formal tones; passive tense used twice.*

Whole class
Ask the group working on OHTs to present answers to the question they have been set.
Does everyone agree with their analysis?

Lesson 2

Whole class

Display the captions from yesterday and show and read out the remaining two letters from Copymasters 45 and 46.
Follow the lesson organisation as yesterday, using these questions for letters C and D.
Follow the same approach for differentiation and feedback from the whole class at the end of the lesson.

Letter C What is the complaint about? Are any reasons given which support the complaint? What are the feelings being expressed? Does the writer expect a reply? Underlying purpose?
Letter D What is the writer trying to persuade the reader to do? How does he/she try to do this? Does the writer expect a reply? Underlying purpose?

Lesson 3

Whole class

Model planning then composing a letter of complaint using the language features from Copymaster 45. This could be linked to a school visit as part of a history trip. Display the Features Card (Copymaster 47) for this type of letter:

• opening sentence states what the complaint is
• following sentences give further reasons to back up the complaint
• angry, emotional tone and phrases, including the letter ending (alternatively this could be formal but assertive).

As you write, re-state the purpose (to complain): You may wish to use the following letter as a basis for your modelled writing.

Dear Manager,

A group of pupils and I recently visited your castle as part of our history project and we were very disappointed by the poor service throughout the day.

We expected the guide we have always used but he had been placed with a different school.

The guide we had spoke so softly we could not hear him, and when some pupils asked him questions he said he had no time to answer them.

Many of the captions on the walls were written in such small print we had great difficulty in reading them. Some were missing completely.

This is not at all what we had expected, and I am expecting a full and immediate response to my letter, with a full refund for every pupil in the group.

What a waste of a day!

J.J. Jones (class teacher).

Group and independent work

Tell pupils to draft a letter of complaint along the same lines linked to a supposedly unsatisfactory visit to their local swimming pool, referring to the Features Card on display. Allow 15 minutes for this and then ask each pupil to exchange their draft letter with another pupil; the response partner checks whether all the correct features are included in the letter.

Differentiation

Low Attainers – Can be given a partially written writing frame.

High Attainers – Will be asked to end their letters without being angry but making it quite clear that they are very unhappy.

Whole class

Ask for feedback on why it is important to use the features of the different letters. Ask some children to read their letters to the class.

Lessons 4 and 5

The purpose of these two lessons is to draft out a letter using one of the four types illustrated, linked to another curriculum area.

This will be for a real purpose, as an outcome of what you have been doing in history, geography, science, art etc.

Each pupil will need the Features Card and a copy of the corresponding letter to model their own letter on. A response partner must check the key features of the letter are in place and that it makes sense; the writer must read aloud the letter to himself/herself to check that punctuation is correct as this is central to the meaning of the letter. Finally, proof-read for any spelling errors.

Each pupil then prepares a final version of the letter. This letter is marked for structure, purpose, meaning/punctuation, spelling and lay out, including handwriting/DTP.

One or all of these letters will be sent off and the reply/replies shared with the class.

Theme 5) Advertisements

Objectives

Text level

- 13 to read and evaluate adverts or fliers, considering:
  - the deliberate use of ambiguity, half-truth, bias;
  - how opinion can be disguised to seem like fact
- 14 to select and evaluate a range of texts for persuasiveness
- 15 from reading, to collect and investigate use of persuasive devices *e.g. words and phrases, rhetorical questions, deliberate ambiguities* and to write examples

Resources

A collection of adverts or fliers, from comics, magazines, newspapers and 'junk-mail', including holiday and car advertisements.

Pictures of cars cut out from car magazines and advertisements, or downloaded from the Internet.
A large, bullet point list of key features of persuasive writing
Copymaster 48 – Advertisements.
Copymaster 49 – Car advertising.
Homework 25.

Assessment

At the end of this theme is the pupil able to:
- detect persuasive language and other effects to realise how the reader is being manipulated to think or act in a certain way;
- use this knowledge to write a car advertisement and prepare a radio advertisement linked to another curriculum area?

Lesson 1

Whole class

Explain to pupils that this theme is about persuasive texts and how they have been written and designed to persuade you to think in a certain way or to do certain things *e.g. to buy their product.*
Put up an advertisement which is large enough for the class to see; read it aloud and ask them to jot down anything they notice under these headings:
- Purpose – to persuade you in some way.
- Layout – what do you look at first and why?
- Information – what is the big message?
- What type of words and phrases have been chosen?
- Opinion – is a view or opinion given as if it is a fact?
- Illustrations – are they effective?
- Use of colour and font – do the choices support the ad?

Ask for feedback on what they have jotted down.

Then ask for their views on whether they consider this to be a successful advert.
Would they change anything?
Ask the class to re-state what the key text features are.

Group and independent work

Now hand out copies of fliers *e.g. for the local leisure centre or for double-glazing.* Ask them to discuss the texts in pairs then use Copymaster 48 to record what they think, quoting from the text to support their views.

Differentiation

Low Attainers – Work with another adult or the teacher.
High Attainers – In pairs, complete Copymaster 48, then role-play a conversation as Person A (who paid for the flier) and Person B (the designer).

Whole class

Selected groups asked to give feedback starting with key features they have observed.

Lesson 2

Whole class

The purpose of today's lesson is to analyse **in more depth** language choice, tense and layout.
Return again to the advertisement and flier used in yesterday's lesson. Focus on each in turn asking the children to respond:
Language choice: Short phrases with no verbs – *Unbeatable Prices; Lifetime Guarantee; Ideal for Women; Friendly and Encouraging Club Atmosphere.* These all stated as the truth – unequivocal, biased to their product.
May have long sentences with 'facts' separated by commas (often found in holiday and car ads).
Adjectives, adverbs, verbs and nouns chosen to compliment the product (painting a good picture).
Lots of exclamation marks to draw attention, giving feel of fun, surprise, enjoyment.
Capitalisation used in mini-headlines
Questions which are not supposed to be answered.
Tense – present tense; often imperatives used.
Layout – may use bullet point lists.

Group and independent work

Hand out a selection of promotional materials and ask pupils independently to circle/underline any of the features focused on in the whole class session and say why they have been used.
Every pupil to find one opinion used as fact.

Differentiation

Low Attainers – Have the texts ready marked up but have to say what they notice.
High Attainers – Select all the opinions and half-truths they can find for *A Half-Truth Handbook,* a guide for writers of promotional and persuasive materials.

Whole class

Ask the class for the results of their survey and the features which seem to appear more often.
Write up the opinions expressed as fact on a sheet and arrange for these to be printed on the computer for a Big Book entitled *A Half-Truth Handbook – a guide for writers of promotional and persuasive materials.*

Summer Term

Lesson 3

Whole class

Explain that the aim today is for pupils to use some of the techniques and features of persuasive texts in designing a car advertisement.

Put up an OHT version of Copymaster 49.

Say that these examples have been selected from a number of car ads.

Read each one in turn and ask for comments linked to discussions from yesterday.

A Sentence begins with *If* which challenges you to take action, followed by an imperative verb *check*, which assumes you will follow this up. A typical bullet point list follows on.

B Note the use of adjectives in order to build up the idea of a carefully crafted car: *beautifully balanced, precision-weighted, deft.*

C Headlines in capitals, phrases used, words left out. Note the use of the verb *boasts* (metaphor).

D Questions used in a conversational way, does not seem to be an advert. Second paragraph aimed to appeal to your vanity.

E Catchy opening phrase. Note the long sentence with key facts separated by commas.

F Sentence starts with *but* – used commonly as if the salesperson is actually speaking to you.

G Punchy and immediate – followed by two authoritative statements. Idiom particularly effective.

Group and independent work

Distribute a number of pictures of cars and copies of Copymaster 49.

Ask each pupil to select a picture and design an advert, modelling their ideas on those included in Copymaster 49.

Each ad must have no more than 50 words.

All pupils work on the same task.

Whole class

Ads to be evaluated by the whole class and the CAR AD OF THE WEEK! selected and displayed.

Lessons 4 and 5

The purpose of this lesson is for pupils to design a radio advert for a place they have studied in geography or history, using the persuasive devices found in the advert. Read the text out (below) and then model the writing of a similar one based on a place you have visited. The structures you must keep are underlined and can be used to scaffold the pupils' own radio ad.

Fancy going somewhere different this summer?

Why not do something different?

Come to Italy *and visit* Rome, *where you can discover at first hand* the splendour and excitement of this city.

We'll guarantee you'll love the Ancient City *and marvel* at the splendid sights.

And that's just the start of your visit: there are so many sensational things to see.

Experience up close encounters with worlds that no longer exist, including centurions who march across the city, gladiators who lunge and scream at their tormentors, the crowd who roars with excitement as the spectacle unfolds, and whose chants echo along the buildings. *And do not forget to share in the feasts that have been carefully prepared, so that you believe you have somehow slipped back into time.*

Group and independent work

Pupils in pairs work on these presentations, using materials from history or geography lessons.

Differentiation

By outcome.

Whole class

Everyone has a draft advert to hand, and these are presented to the class, or possibly in the hall using a microphone, to create authenticity.

These are evaluated and an audio tape made for use at presentations and for future reference by next year's class.

Theme 6) Persuasion

Mixed ability groups throughout this unit in order to share ideas and opinions.

Objectives

Text level
- 14 to select and evaluate a range of texts, in print or other media, for persuasiveness
- 19 to construct an argument in note form or full text to persuade others of a point of view and:
  - present the case to the class or group
  - evaluate its effectiveness

Resources
A range of texts from other subject areas, including video, software, songs, poetry, photographs: history, geography, science, art, religious education, where a point of view is being expressed to persuade the reader to think in a certain way.
Music by The Beatles (*Eleanor Rigby*); Peter, Paul and Mary (*If I had a Hammer*).

Listening centre and headphones; TV and video.
Magazine photographs which express a strong point of view.
Number fans.
Copymasters 50 and 51. Homework 26.

Assessment
At the end of this theme is the pupil able to:
- detect a point of view expressed in a range of different materials;
- express and justify his/her views;
- evaluate the validity of his/her views;
- present a point of view orally, using an argument frame as support;
- evaluate the quality of his/her point of view/argument and the way it was presented?

Lessons 1 and 2

Whole class

Explain to the class that they are going to be involved in some detective work!
The next two lessons will be spent in a carousel of activities, whose sole purpose is as follows.
Through reading (printed text), watching (films/videos), studying (photographs, especially propaganda materials) and listening to songs (folk songs, songs which recount something and/or express a view) they must work out what the point of view is and how effective the writer/film maker/song writer/artist is in getting his/her message across and persuading the reader listener to think in a certain way.

To help pupils, display a large version of copymaster 50 with the first answer covered up. Play the song *If I had a Hammer* and ask the children for their views. They can jot these down on their whiteboards. Tell them that you have summarised their views and reveal the answer on the copymaster. Now do the same for the second box on the copymaster. Read aloud *Whalesong* and ask the children to write down what it is about.

Group and independent work
In mixed ability groups, use a carousel approach so that pupils experience a variety of persuasive materials.
All the pupils are given a selection of materials and asked to decide what the point of view is.
Their views are filled in on Copymaster 50.

Lesson 3

Whole class

Pupils bring their filled in Copymaster 50 to this lesson. In pairs, pupils select one example of materials they have worked on and put forward their opinions on what point of view is being expressed. This may involve:
- playing a video extract or a CD Rom
- displaying a magazine photograph
- reading aloud a text
- playing a soundtrack or a song

- acting out a scene from a play
The rest of the class agree/disagree.
Pupils then vote on the effectiveness of the materials in expressing a point of view by using a number fan, giving it a rating up to 5.
The teacher adds up the scores quickly and gives it an 'average rating'.
At the end of Lesson 3 the highest scoring materials are displayed on a stand in Gold, Silver and Bronze positions.

Lessons 4

Whole class

Explain to the class that another way to persuade people is through a spoken presentation e.g. in a debate or meeting.

Put up a large version of copymaster 51. Fill in one as on the sample which follows, using their suggestions.

Copymaster 51   Argument Frame

Name: *Class 5*

Date: *13/7/01*

We believe that *schools should provide breakfast.*

There are several reasons which support our view. To begin with there is evidence that *many children come to school hungry because they get up late and have no time to eat.*

Furthermore, we know that *parents often do not have time to prepare breakfast for their children because they are rushing off to work.*

Moreover, it has been proved that *breakfast is important because it is more difficult to work hard and think carefully on an empty stomach!*

Therefore, although some people think that *schools should not offer breakfast.*

We think that we have shown, without any doubt, that *they should if they want pupils to perform better and get higher marks in exams.*

Lesson 5

Whole class

This is a real challenge for pupils, because today they must take the arguments frames from yesterday and present the opposite point of view.

Pupils prepare their frames and again present their views.

Give out blank copies of this copymaster for children to fill in.

Ask pupils to suggest topics they feel strongly about: e.g. *Schools should provide breakfast; Schools should allow more time for drama and games; School uniform should be banned; Homework should be banned in primary school; Pupils should have total freedom to explore the Internet; Girls and boys should be treated equally.*

Ask pupils to choose a topic from the list and divide the class up into groups with the same topics.

Ask them to brainstorm some of the points they would make in their argument

Group and independent work

Pupils fill in an argument frame incorporating the points they wish to make, starting with an opening statement of viewpoint, backing this up by several more points and making a concluding statement aimed at convincing the audience that this is a 'watertight' view, not to be contradicted in any way.

Use Copymaster 51 for this, or they can design one for themselves.

Use of voice, eye contact and gesture are important to support their views.

Whole class

Choose a selection of pupils to present their arguments, the class evaluating the quality of the arguments using number fans up to 5.

Ask the class to evaluate the success of these arguments and to vote using number fans.

Ask them to discuss why this activity was more difficult then the one from yesterday.

Theme 7) Using dictionaries

Objectives

Vocabulary extension:
- 10 to use a range of dictionaries and understand their purposes
- 12 to use dictionaries efficiently to explore spellings, meanings, derivations
- 13 to compile own class/group dictionary using personally written definitions *e.g. of slang, technical terms*

Resources

A range of children's dictionaries and thesauruses; adult dictionaries. Set of wordcards beginning with every letter of the alphabet
Set of synonym cards for a 'pairs' game (use words from synonym homework sheet).

A list of key words from a different subject area.
Copymaster 52 – Spelling and definitions.
Copymaster 53 – Slang.
Homework 27.

Assessment

At the end of this theme is the pupil able to:
- use a range of dictionaries confidently by using alphabetical order, abbreviations and definitions with understanding;
- select the correct dictionary for the job in hand;
- find out the origins of words;
- extend his/her vocabulary through regular and expert use of dictionaries?

Lesson 1

Whole class

Explain that this theme is all about using different dictionaries for different purposes. This lesson is about using them efficiently to check spelling and word meanings. Have ready a collection of children's dictionaries, one each, if possible.

The Quartiles of a dictionary: Ask pupils to open the dictionary at about the centre – what letter(s) have they found? Now ask them to find the half way point between the beginning and the centre – what letter(s) have they found? Finally ask them to find the half way point between the centre and the end of the dictionary – what letter(s) have they found?
Repeat this at speed, getting them to open the dictionary at different quartiles.
Now see how quickly they can find different letters within the quartiles. Ask the children how they think this activity will help them to use dictionaries.
Headers and footers: give them a header word and its matching footer word *e.g. lively* and *love.* Ask them to tell you where these words are found.
Tell them how to use them: look at the headers and

footers **first** when looking up a word in order to locate the right section; **then** skim down the appropriate page until you find the word you want.
Checking spelling – write up a few words, some misspelled, and ask them to check the spelling.

Group and independent work

In pairs, give pupils 1 minute to practise finding quartiles and 4 minutes to find words, turning over a card from a shuffled set of cards on the table.
Write up a list of *headers and footers*, then get them to write down page numbers.
Using Copymaster 52, get them to check spellings and definitions.

Differentiation

Low Attainers – Can have more time for the first two activities, and use a simpler dictionary for checking some spellings and meanings you have given them.
High Attainers – Can use dictionaries efficiently and so can use an adult dictionary.

Whole class

Ask a number of pupils to read out Copymaster 52, the rest of the class checking their answers.

Lesson 2

Whole class

Say that looking up derivations is interesting as it offers us a picture of languages that were once spoken in our country, or words which were borrowed from other countries and which have entered our language
Demonstrate how to find out where a word is derived from by enlarging sections from an adult dictionary *e.g.*
Comb – *(Old English* **camb***; related to Old Norse* **kambr***, Old High German* **camb***)*

Group and independent work

Some suggested words for this activity: *mare, need, orange, cramp, grub, idol, many, pilfer, shoe, zero.*
Give each group 3 words to look up; then ask them to

write each word on a large piece of card and one old word + one language of origin on the back, *e.g.*

comb		cambr Old Norse

Differentiation

Low Attainers – A set of cards used in yesterday's lesson and practise finding words quickly in a dictionary.
High Attainers – Complete the same task as the rest of the class.

Whole class

Ask what they have learned from this activity.

Lesson 3

Whole class

Pupils will need the homework sheets on synonyms and antonyms from previous themes.

Explain that this lesson will look at the difference between thesauruses and a dictionary of antonyms and synonyms. Demonstrate what the difference is: a thesaurus offers meanings, the other dictionary just a series of alternatives, either antonyms or synonyms. Ask which is more useful.

When writing, you will need definitions to ensure your choice of words is correct. In this case a thesaurus would be appropriate. If you are just looking for a list of synonyms, a synonym/antonym dictionary would be best.

Group and independent work

Ask one half of the class to use their synonym homework sheet and the other half of the class to use their antonym homework sheet. Pupils work in pairs.

Those with the synonyms sheets brainstorm a list of antonyms, and vice versa for the other group.
Pupils work in pairs against the clock then use the rest of the session dictionaries to find some more – the winning pair has the most words!

Differentiation

Low Attainers – Play a pairs game on synonyms, turning over cards until they find a pair.
High Attainers – Design an antonym and synonym Hangman game for the class *e.g.*
This word is the opposite of open (closed). This word is similar in meaning to attractive (pretty). This word is the opposite of friendly (spiteful). This word is similar in meaning to heavy (weighty).

Whole class

Ask the high attaining group to play the Hangman game they have designed with the whole class.

Lesson 4

Whole class

Choose a subject area *e.g. history, maths or science* and display a list of words which are used regularly in this subject. Choose those words which pupils have difficulty in remembering/understanding/spelling. Arrange them alphabetically.

Model how to write a definition then ask the children to give you their definition for another word, and write this up. If you were using mathematical words, you could use the following examples:
Diameter: a line drawn from one side of a circle to the other passing through the centre.
Hexagon: a shape with six sides.

Group and independent work

Divide the list up between the groups and ask them to discuss definitions, then use a dictionary to check meanings. Each group should produce a neatly written card, each of the same size. One group has responsibility for sticking them into a Big Book in the right order and designing a contents list and a cover on the computer.
Title: *Our Big Book of Key Words for Maths.*

Differentiation

All pupils work on the same task.

Whole class

The book is displayed. Ask pupils why it is useful to create a dictionary like this.

Lesson 5

Whole class

Explain to the class that the aim is to create a Dictionary of Slang. These are words which young people use amongst themselves to their friends. Often, parents or other adults cannot understand the meaning of slang – ask why this is.

Group and independent work

Hand out Copymaster 53 and ask them to tick the word if it is still in fashion, then update the list. Independently, each pupil produces a mini slang dictionary of their own using folded paper.

It must be in alphabetical order.
Definitions may be given if necessary, or a code produced to indicate those words which are similar in meaning.
Point out that this could be another synonyms dictionary.
No differentiation – all pupils do the same task.

Whole class

Ask a few pupils to say why slang words are used, and ask pupils in pairs to produce an impromptu conversation in which slang is used.

Theme 8) Poetry

Objectives

Text level
- 3 to change point of view
- 4 to read rehearse and modify performance of poetry
- 7 to write from another character's point of view
- 19 to construct an argument in note form or full text to persuade others of a point of view

Resources
Copymasters 54, 55 and 56.
A jazz cassette with some good trumpet playing.
Homework 28.

Assessment
At the end of this theme is the pupil able to:
- stand back from a text and evaluate the views that are being expressed;
- organise and present an argument effectively;
- deliver an effective and polished performance of a poem?

Lesson 1

Whole class

Read aloud the poem *Benny McEever* by Gareth Owen (Copymasters 54, 55 and 56).
Give the whole class two minutes' time out; ask one third of the class to jot down their views on Benny, another third their views on his gran, and the remaining third their views on his dad.
Ask the class to share their views with you.
Write up the three names of these characters and make a bullet point list of pupils' views.

Group and independent work
Give out a sheet of paper with three blank speech bubbles, and ask each pupil to write something in each bubble as if one of these characters was saying something about their lives.
All pupils do the same activity.

Whole class
Ask pupils to read out a selection of the speech bubbles and ask the class what view of the character is being given.

Lesson 2

Whole class/group work

Hand out copies of the poem to trios of pupils and ask them to choose one of the key events in the poem to *produce a **freeze-frame*** – pupils prepare a key event and on the word 'freeze' hold the image for a few seconds – *e.g. children moving away from Barry as he walks down the street; stealing the watch; Benny showing the watch to a fellow pupil.* Tell them that you will be tapping each pupil on the shoulder as they hold the Freeze-Frame – this will signal that the character must speak aloud his/her thoughts.

Allow 20 minutes for this.
Group all the pupils in a circle and ask each group to produce their freeze frame while the class guesses which event it represents.
As the pupils hold the image, ask a pupil to tap each pupil on the shoulder in turn and ask him/her to think aloud his/her thoughts at that moment e.g. **Barry:** *'I hate school – they all hate me';* first pupil from his school: *'He's horrible – smelly ugh!';* second pupil from his school: *'I feel sorry for him – I've seen where he lives and it's disgusting!'*
Ask all pupils to present their freeze-frame, the other pupils commenting on the effectiveness of the image.

Lesson 3

Whole class

Ask pupils why the poet has painted such a bleak image of Benny. Remind them that their freeze-frames offered a number of negative images of Benny.

Say that the purpose of this lesson is to present an argument to a reader of this poem on the reasons for Benny's behaviour, trying to persuade him/her to change possible negative views about Benny.

Group work

Ask pupils in pairs to produce notes in a chart like the one below. Finish it, then give them a blank argument frame and ask pupils individually to write in their views.

Differentiation

Low Attainers – Are given the notes about Benny already filled in.

High Attainers – Could incorporate the argument as part of a letter from a pupil who feels sorry for Benny to a school governor.

Whole class

Ask selected pupils to present their arguments/letters orally, pupils giving critical feedback on the quality of their arguments.

Collect in the notes and mark the arguments for:
• The effective use of the notes
• Text features of a typical argument: *Some people might argue that . . . but I think that . . . To begin with . . . Furthermore . . .*

Benny's life	The effect on him
He never knew his mother	Must have felt unloved
His Dad lived in a cardboard box somewhere	Must have felt unloved – dad never visited
Holes in his shoes	Felt embarrassed
Didn't have any toys	
Had a cornet mouthpiece	

Lessons 4 and 5

Whole class

These lessons will be used to:
• Prepare a polished performance of the poem
• Prepare a set of questions for a pupil in role as 'Benny McEever, the famous jazz musician from London, who overcame an unhappy early life to become one of the world's greatest trumpet players'
• Select a piece of jazz which has some good trumpet playing on it
• Rehearse and present this to another class/parents.

Explain that the aim is to present a chat show interview of Benny McEever.

He will walk into the class to the sound of some jazz trumpet playing.

As this fades away, he will sit down to be interviewed about his present success and his early life by pupils who have prepared a set of questions on cards.

The interview will end as Benny McEever walks off to the notes of his own trumpet playing.

The rest of the class will then present the poem, carefully rehearsed.

Group work

Divide the class up into groups of pupils who will perform the poem, and those who will prepare questions on cards.

Performing the poem

The poem is written with alternate rhyming lines: *feet, street; rocks, box;* pupils must decide how to present this. Suggestions might be:
• A choral version set to a 'rap' type beat
• Divided into sections with individual or pairs of voices
• Arrangement of pupils – a 'tight' group or a semi-circle.

Pupils decide how they will present it and rehearse it together, the teacher offering critical feedback.

Writing the question cards

Pupils can use their notes from yesterday to design a set of questions. Each pair can be given different sections of the poem, and prepare them in draft form first.

As a whole group they need to come together to check that no questions have been asked twice.

When this has happened, pupils can prepare the question cards.

Pupils should nominate who is to play Benny McEever (or you could do this).

One or two pupils need to select a piece of music and arrange the chairs for the interview.

Once the pupils have run through this twice, they should be ready to perform.

Theme 9) 'Classics'

Objectives

Text level

- 6 to explore the challenge and appeal of older literature through:
  - listening to older literature being read aloud
  - reading accessible poems, stories and extracts
  - reading extracts from classic serials shown on television
  - discussing differences in language used
- 8 to record predictions, questions, reflections, while reading
- 9 to write in the style of the author

Resources

The Puffin Book of Twentieth-Century Children's Stories; The Secret Garden and *The Little Princess* by Frances Hodgson Burnett; *The Railway Children* by E. Nesbit; *The Chronicles of Narnia* by C.S. Lewis; *Usborne Book of Children's Classics – graphic versions; Poems from Dark as a Midnight Dream* by Fiona Walters; *The Graphic Shakespeare Series –* *Macbeth, The Tempest, A Midsummer Night's Dream;* video material of classics.
A definition of the word 'classic' ready prepared on paper.
Whiteboards and pens.
Copymaster 57.
Copymaster 58.
Homework 29.

Assessment

At the end of this theme is the pupil able to:

- identify the features of 'classics' and discuss these with confidence;
- enjoy and appreciate 'classics' through hearing extracts read aloud or through his/her own personal reading;
- understand the different uses of language in 'classics' in comparison with modern versions on the same theme;
- create dialogue which matches the style of a 'classic' author;
- record his/her views on a text and write a commentary?

Lesson 1

Whole class

Watch a short extract from a film or video version of a classic novel then read out an extract from the book. Explain to the class that the book is regarded as a 'classic' – ask the class what classic might mean relating to what they have just heard read aloud. After they have shared their ideas put up the definition – how close were they?
Classic: timeless, long lasting appeal, generally agreed to be very good, a book my parents read and I've read it too ...

Group and independent work

Give out Copymaster 57, with titles of many books which are considered classics.

Ask pupils in groups to tick off or highlight any classic books they have read; in turn these pupils explain to the group why they think this book is a classic

Differentiation

Low Attainers – Complete the same task as the rest of the class.
High Attainers – Are asked to see if they can make any links between the books e.g. *same genre (adventure); same kind of problems (heroes have to win over enemy).*

Whole class

Pupils to give 1-minute presentations on *What Makes this Book a Classic.*

Lesson 2

Whole class

Read aloud the whole of a first chapter of a classic book.
Ask pupils to make notes about characters, setting, plot and what they liked. (This could be further developed for homework or personal reading journals using Copymaster 58.)

Group and independent work

Ask pupils to write a commentary using their notes on the writing frame if necessary.
Give them a simple writing frame:

Characters
In this first chapter we are introduced to ....

Setting
The story is set ....
Problem/Plot
This is introduced when.......
Problem/Plot
This is not yet introduced but we can probably predict that........
What I liked *about the book was ....*

Differentiation

Low Attainers – Can be given some ready made notes in order to complete their frame.
High Attainers – Can write a commentary in the first person from a main character's point of view, building in all the relevant points.

Whole class

Read out several commentaries and ask pupils to note down common threads typical of classic books.

Lesson 3

Tell the class that they will be looking at two classic poems, then looking at the different language used in comparison with two other poems on the same theme.

Read out two classic poems with similar themes *e.g. Home Thoughts from Abroad – Robert Browning; I know a bank where the wild thyme blows – A Midsummer Night's Dream.*

Ask pupils why they think these are regarded as classics and often found in collections/anthologies – what gives them the timeless quality. Is there any similarity between classic stories and classic poetry?

Group and independent work

Give each group some modern poems with the same theme – the beauty of nature/seasons *e.g. It is Snowing by Afua Cooperor or I So Liked Spring by Charlotte Mew.*

In pairs, ask them to make notes about differences in the language used in the classic versions and the modern ones. Each group should make a list with paper divided into two (as below).

Differentiation

Low Attainers – Are supported in reading the classic poems.
High Attainers – Discuss whether the modern poems might one day be considered classics. Ask them to make a bullet point list. Their ideas will be used to begin the final lesson.

Whole class

Ask all groups for some examples of the differences in language and style used in the poems, reflecting on the objective.

Classic poems (examples of words & phrases; style)	Modern Poems (examples of words & phrases; style)

Lesson 4

Whole class

Say that today the aim is to add another piece of dialogue into the extract from a classic book you are just about to read.

Read out an extract from *The Lion, the Witch and the Wardrobe* where Edmund meets the Queen.

Ask the pupils to put themselves in the position of the Queen who knows nothing about boys. Ask all the pupils to make a quick list of things boys like doing.

The aim is to insert some more dialogue in after the sentence *He was too confused by this time to understand what the question meant.*

Say that you want three more pieces of dialogue before the words *I see you are an idiot.*

The Queen will start each piece of dialogue and Edmund gives three examples of what boys like doing, in order to give her some understanding. She will probably be very aggressive and ask for explanations *e.g.*

'Tell me! What are you?' yelled the Queen.
'I am a boy and . . . I like playing football' said Edmund.

Edmund must remain timid as in the extract.

Group and independent work

Independently pupils draft out this piece of dialogue.

Differentiation

Low Attainers – Can be given a partially completed frame to complete.
High Attainers – Complete the same task.

Whole class

Ask for several pairs of pupils to say their lines out loud, role-playing the characters.

Ask pupils to decide whether they have kept to C.S. Lewis' style.

Lesson 5

Whole class

Start off this lesson by the high attaining group sharing their ideas in a bullet point list on whether the modern poems could be considered classics.

Show them Copymaster 57 again and say that the aim is to create a *Modern Classics* sheet to display in the entrance hall of school.

First they need to brainstorm a list of book titles which they consider will still be read in 50 years' time. They should refer to the list the group has just displayed and the original definition.

Group and independent work

Mix all the groups up so that there will be some widely read pupils in each group.

Each group comes up with ideas for titles and then the group decides whether or not to include it as a classic. Ask them to write their titles on card.

Whole class

Each group in turn comes to the front and displays their cards; different members of the group present their views.

All groups have a turn.

The class makes a final decision on each title; you type these into a table on screen. This is printed and copied and each pupil takes a sheet home (basis for homework sheet).

One of these sheets is displayed in the entrance hall with the caption *Your child voted for these books as tomorrow's classics!*

Theme 10 Grammar

Objectives

• 1 to secure the basic conventions of standard English Sentence construction and punctuation
• 6 to investigate clauses through:
   • identifying the main clause in a long sentence investigating sentences which have more than one clause
   • understanding how clauses are connected *e.g. by combining three short sentences into one*

Resources

A washing line with these conjunctions pegged on it: so, but, when, as, while, before, after, since, until, if, because, although, that, and, or:

Copymaster 59 – Sentences
Copymaster 60 – Joining 3 sentences.
Homework 30.

Assessment

At the end of this theme is the pupil able to:
• understand what a main clause is and identify the main clause in a sentence;
• extend sentences by adding conjunctions;
• investigate texts to find three common uses of the comma;
• use commas effectively in his/her own sentences to improve the quality of his/her writing?

Lesson 1

Whole class

Explain to the class that the aim of the lesson is to identify a main clause in a sentence.
All main clauses must have a subject and a verb.
Write up the sentence: *He drank tea.* And ask *Who drank tea? He drank tea* (underline the subject). *What did he do? He drank.* Now underline the verb in a different colour. *He drank tea.* Subject = *He*; verb = *drank.*
He drank is the main clause.
The additional word *tea* completes the sentence, telling us what he drank; however, the main clause could stand alone and make sense.
Write up *She sipped her wine. Who sipped her wine? She sipped her wine. What did she do? She sipped her wine.*
Subject = *She*; verb = *sipped.*
Now get the class to work on the following clauses in the same way: *Alex loved milkshakes. Everyone liked Oscar.*

Quickly say some sentences and ask them to identify the main clause: *The salmon leapt from the river. Grandpa liked strolling in the park. She played the trumpet.*

Group and independent work

Hand out the first five sentences from Copymaster 59 and ask the pupils to identify the main clause.

Differentiation

Low Attainers – Are given the main clause and the remaining words which are then added in by them to make sense.
High Attainers – Delete the main clause and see if they can replace it with another one which makes sense.

Whole class

Ask for the main clauses from each sentence.
Ask pupils why it is useful to be able to identify the main clause in a sentence.

Lesson 2

Whole class

Tell the class that you are going to add in another clause to the sentence by adding a conjunction. Remind them of the work they have already done on this on Copymaster 26.
Peg up all the conjunctions on the washing line.
Explain that adding conjunctions makes sentences more interesting. Demonstrate how to do this.

Group and independent work

Distribute the sentence beginnings from Copymaster 59.

Ask pupils to write endings by choosing a conjunction and an ending (subordinate clause) which makes sense. All pupils complete the same task.

Whole class

Tell pupils to remain in their groups; ask 3 pupils to read out their complete sentences.
Now collect in their endings, re-distribute them to the groups, and ask a selection of pupils to read them out now.
Ask the class to vote on the silliest/funniest sentence.

Lesson 3

Whole class

The aim of the lesson is to join three sentences together with conjunctions then use this opening line for a mini-story.

Use Copymaster 60 as an OHT and ask pupils to choose suitable conjunctions from the washing line. Write these up where pupils can see them.

Independent work

Every pupil can now choose a sentence as the introduction to a mini-story of no more than 50 words.

Pupils edit and proof-read carefully checking that this is written in standard English:

• Agreement between nouns and verbs
• Consistency of tense and subject
• Avoidance of double negatives
• Avoidance of non-standard dialect words.

Whole class

Work is marked for the correct features of standard English as well as for spelling and punctuation.

Lessons 4 and 5

Whole class

Start off this session by enjoying some of the mini-stories by copying several on to OHT or by asking pupils to read theirs to the class.

Go on to explain that you are now going to be detective readers and pick out sentences where the comma has been used in different ways, within sentences.

Refer to previous work on punctuation in both grammar themes from the previous terms.

Demonstrate the 3 sentences below, explaining their structure as summarised in the brackets. Now ask them to look for examples of sentences punctuated exactly like those below. Use fiction and non-fiction books.

1. *I started to do my homework, but couldn't concentrate.* (Two main clauses separated by a comma.)
2. *She packed two black skirts, two belts, two tunics, two pairs of white socks and two pairs of ballet shoes.* (Main clause followed by a list of other items; each separated by a comma except the last two items.)
3. *Many urban buildings, such as office blocks, are quite ugly.* (Main clause separated by a pair of commas enclosing extra information.)

Group and independent work

When pairs of children have found an example of each of these three types, ask them to write a different sentence, copying the use of punctuation but writing about something different.

Use a whole class writing session to demonstrate this:

1. *I started to eat my supper, but didn't feel hungry.*
2. *He packed his shorts, trainers, socks, shirt and a Mars bar.*
3. *Some wild animals, such as foxes, have become tame.*

Differentiation

Low Attainers – Select sentences from easier texts.

High Attainers – Write about how the comma helps to make meaning within the writing.

Ask all pupils to check their five last pieces of writing for the use of commas within the sentence.

If they cannot find an example, they must change a sentence, copying one of the three types.

Explain that they will become better writers if they do this.

Whole class

Review all five lessons, asking pupils to reflect on what they have learned and how they can apply it to their own writing.

A visit to London

Last Friday my whole class went to London.

When we arrived the first thing we saw was the 'London Eye' – the huge wheel which was recently erected. We all walked past it and took photographs – it was moving so slowly we thought it had broken down.

After walking past the 'Eye' we travelled to the London Aquarium, because we were studying underwater life as part of our Science topic.

Before lunch we saw porpoises and sea lions, octopuses and amazing giant sand worms which seemed to look at us as we walked past.

During lunch we watched a video on the dangers to creatures which live in the sea.

In the afternoon we saw some animals being fed.

When we returned home we were exhausted but happy because we had learnt so much and had a good time too.

A sports report

23 all out is record Barnes low

Barnes made a record start
to the second division campaign
as they were bowled out for just 23.

A side with a long-time reputation
for batting prowess found Merton's
bowling all too much on a damp pitch.

The team missed the support of
leading batsmen Tony Day
(holiday) and Tom Parker (broken arm).
Barnes failed to get near the home team's 39.
It was the lowest score in both first
divisions of the league.

Spokesman Alasdair Walsh said:
'It was a pretty difficult pitch, and the
fact that we were missing our best
players did not help.'
As the players left the field they were
clapped by home supporters.

Playscripts

A play with five characters:

Les
Tim
Liz
Miss
Sir

and a chorus: All (the class).

Outside

Les   Hey, you!
Tim   Who? Me?
Les   You I'm talking to. You.
Tim   What?
Les   Who do you think you're staring at?
Tim   You what?
Les   Who do you think you're looking at?
Tim   I'm not looking at anybody.
Les   You are. You're looking at me.
Tim   I'm not
Les   You are. You're doing it now.
Tim   Only 'cause you shouted. I wasn't looking before.
Les   You were. You were staring.
Tim   I wasn't.
Les   You were.
Tim   I wasn't.
Les   Are you calling me a liar?

Tim   No.
Les   You are.
Tim   I'm just telling you. I'm just saying, I wasn't looking at you. Honest.
Les   So you're saying I'm a liar, then.
Tim   No.
Les   You'd better watch who you're calling a liar.
Tim   I'm not.
Les   You'd better look out, that's all.
Tim   What for?
Les   For me. You'd better look out for me.
Tim   You said I hadn't to.
Les   What?
Tim   Look at you.
Les   Are you trying to be funny?
Tim   No.
Les   Don't try to be funny with me.
Tim   I wasn't. It was just a joke.
Les   You'll not be laughing when I've finished with you.
Tim   I'm not laughing. Who's laughing? I'm not.
Les   You'll be laughing on the other side of your face. You don't mess with Les.
Tim   Eh?
Les   You don't mess with Les. What you grinning at?
Tim   I'm not. It's just the way my mouth is.
Les   Right. Down the dene after school.
Tim   Which dene?
Les   What do you mean, which dene? The dene.
Tim   I don't go home that way.
Les   You'd better be there.
Tim   I've got the bus to catch.
Les   Be there!
Tim   Right!
Les   Right!

Playscripts

In the classroom

Liz   Are you all right?

Tim   Who? Me?

Liz   You look pale.

Tim   Do I? No, I'm all right.

Liz   You look ill.

Tim   Well, I feel a bit sick.

Liz   Thought you said you were all right.

Tim   I am. Apart from feeling sick.

Liz   You should ask to go home.

Tim   Home?

Liz   Home. Where you live. What's the matter with you?

Tim   You mean go home early?

Liz   Of course.

Tim   That's a good idea.

Liz   Right.

Tim   Only she wouldn't let me.

Liz   She might. No harm in asking. Miss?

Miss   Yes?

Liz   Tim wants to ask you summat.

Miss   Tim wants to ask me something.

Liz   That's what I said. Tim wants to ask you summat.

Miss   Let him speak for himself. What is it, Tim?

Tim   Nothing, Miss.

Miss   Oh.

Liz   Ask him how he feels, Miss.

Miss   How do you feel, Tim?

Tim   I feel sick, Miss.

Miss   Well, open a window

Tim   What if somebody's walking underneath?

from *Right!* by David Williams

Writing an explanation based on a flowchart

Put these points in the correct order for a flow chart, then write one paragraph of information as an explanation.

A river's journey

River meets sea

Downstream river widens and curves

Many small streams lower down meet up to make a river

Small streams high up

River carves steep valley upstream

Different openings

'Your Auntie Betty has copped it,' said Pa Hedgehog to Ma.
'Oh, no!' cried Ma. 'Where?'
'Just down the road. Opposite the newsagent's. Bad place to cross, that.'
'Everywhere's a bad place to cross nowadays,' said Ma. 'The traffic's dreadful. Do you realise,
Pa, that's the third this year, and all on my side of the family too. First there was grandfather,
then my second cousin once removed, and now poor old Auntie Betty…'

from *The Hodgeheg* by Dick King-Smith

Here is Howard.
He likes
roller skating,
watching TV
and doing
difficult jigsaws.
Favourite smell:
fried onions.
Favourite taste:
peanut butter.

This is Howard's
sister, Alice.
She collects things –
pebbles,
china ornaments
and Anything Pink.
She plays tennis
and basketball
(but not at
the same time).

from *Hooray for Howard* by Colin West

Dark spruce forest frowned on either side the frozen waterway. The trees had been stripped
by a recent wind of their white covering of frost, and they seemed to lean toward each other,
black and ominous, in the fading light. A vast silence reigned over the land. The land itself was
a desolation, lifeless, without movement, so lone and cold that the spirit of it was not even that
of sadness. There was a hint in it of laughter, but of a laughter more terrible than any sadness
– a laughter that was mirthless as the smile of the sphinx, a laughter cold as the frost and
partaking of the grimness of infallibility. It was the masterful and incommunicable wisdom of
eternity laughing at the futility of life and the effort of life. It was the Wild – the savage,
frozen-hearted Northland Wild.

from *White Fang* by Jack London

| Setting | Character | Dialogue |

Flow charts

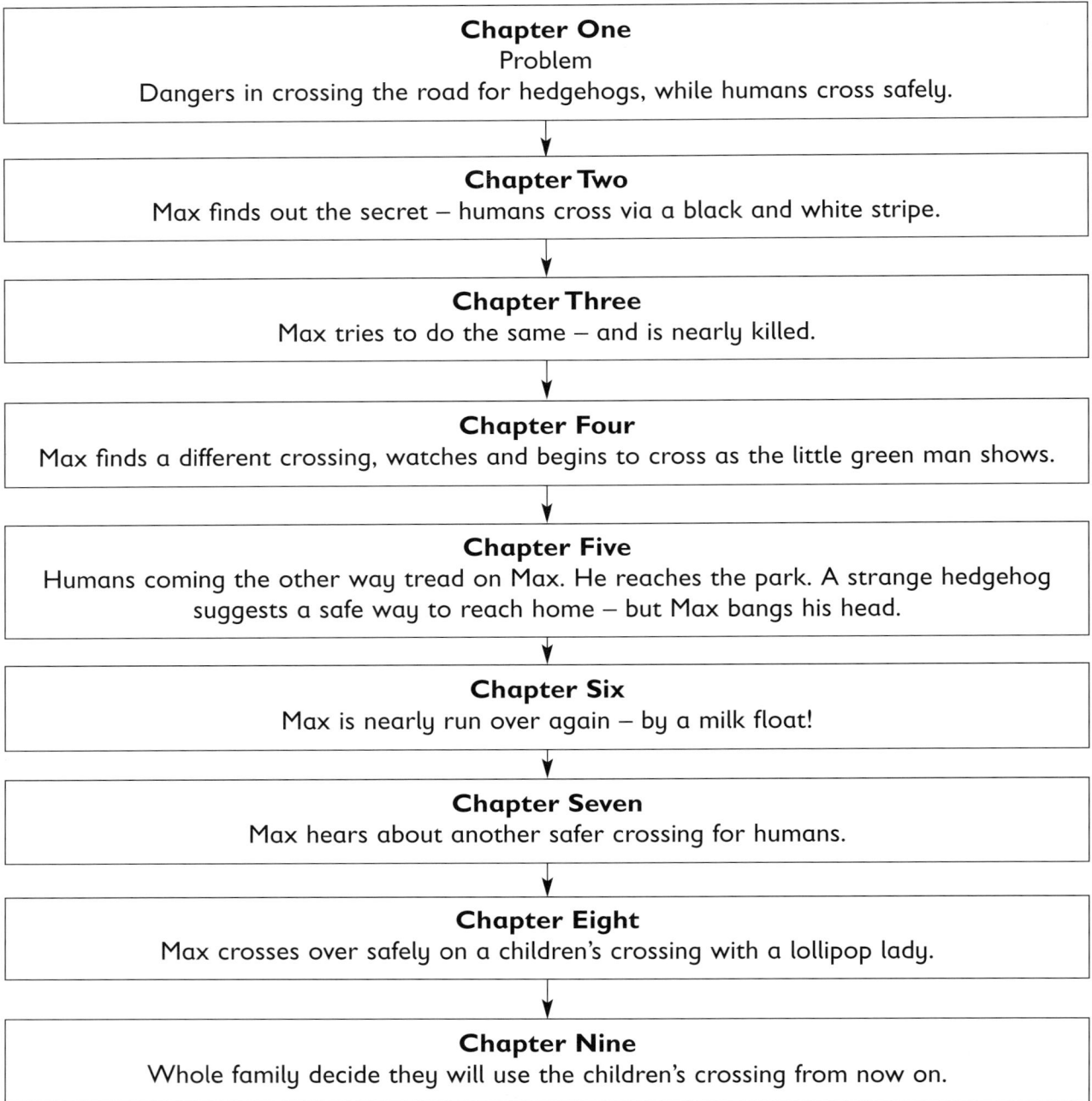

| **Chapter One** |
| Problem |
| Dangers in crossing the road for hedgehogs, while humans cross safely. |

↓

| **Chapter Two** |
| Max finds out the secret – humans cross via a black and white stripe. |

↓

| **Chapter Three** |
| Max tries to do the same – and is nearly killed. |

↓

| **Chapter Four** |
| Max finds a different crossing, watches and begins to cross as the little green man shows. |

↓

| **Chapter Five** |
| Humans coming the other way tread on Max. He reaches the park. A strange hedgehog suggests a safe way to reach home – but Max bangs his head. |

↓

| **Chapter Six** |
| Max is nearly run over again – by a milk float! |

↓

| **Chapter Seven** |
| Max hears about another safer crossing for humans. |

↓

| **Chapter Eight** |
| Max crosses over safely on a children's crossing with a lollipop lady. |

↓

| **Chapter Nine** |
| Whole family decide they will use the children's crossing from now on. |

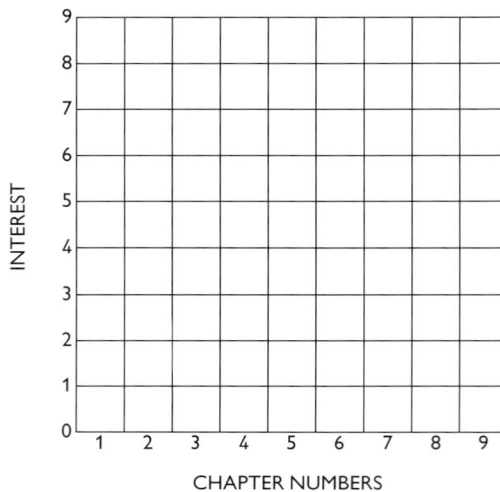

CHAPTER NUMBERS

Fiction characters

Appearance

Actions

Feelings

Fiction characters

What the author wants you to feel

What the author wants you to feel

What the author wants you to feel

Book reviews

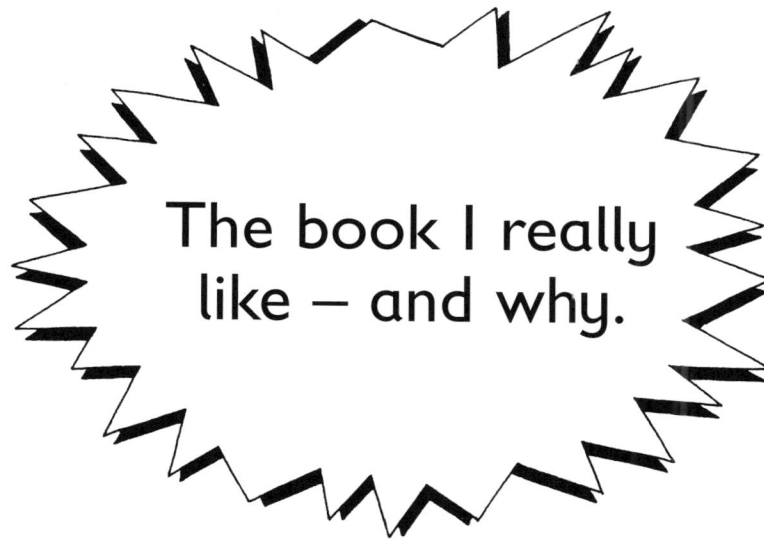

The book I really like – and why.

Title:

Author:

Type of story:

What I liked about it:
   Characters
   Humour
   Action
   Setting
   Style of writing

Examples from text on pages _____
and _____

Back cover blurbs

Friend or Foe – Michael Morpurgo

'What do we do?' Tucky whispered.
'We got to help him, haven't we?
He saved your life, you owe him,
Davey. We both do.'

The Germans are bombing London.
Every day people are dying in the Blitz.
Everyone hates the Germans — especially David:
they killed his father. And now, because of them,
David and Tucky have been evacuated, sent
away to the country to live with strangers.

So when a German soldier rescues David from
drowning, and then asks *him* for help, David is
faced with a terrible dilemma ...

An exciting and moving war-time story from the
author of *Mr Nobody's Eyes*, *Why the Whales
Came* and *Waiting for Anya*.

Boy – Roald Dahl

**Throughout my young days at school and
just afterwards, a number of things
happened to me ... Some are funny. Some
are painful. Some are unpleasant ... all
are true.**

Many remarkable things did happen to Roald
Dahl when he was a boy, no doubt providing
some of the marvellous ideas for his later books.
And, like his stories, Dahl's childhood tales are
unmissable.

'A brilliantly coloured, sometimes grotesque and
sometimes magical world' – *Sunday Times*

The Jungle Books – Rudyard Riping

EDITED WITH AN INTRODUCTION BY DANIEL KARLIN

*'... the torrent of black horns, foaming
muzzles, and staring eyes whirled down the
ravine ... the terrible charge of the buffalo
herd against which no tiger can hope to
stand ...'*

Kipling never visited the jungles of Central India,
yet his descriptions have a breathtaking
imaginative power, and in Mowgli, the boy who
grows up among wolves, he created one of the
most popular and enduring of modern literary
myths. Mowgli's companions and enemies
include such unforgettable creatures as Shere
Khan, the tiger, and Bagheera, the black
panther. From the moment 'a little naked cub'
wanders into the lair of Father Wolf and Mother
Wolf to the moment when the 'Master of the
Jungle' returns to his own people, Mowgli's
adventures comprise a rich and complex fable of
human life. Along with these stories are other
animal tales, ranging from the simple heroism of
'Rikki-tikki-tavi' to the macabre comedy of 'The
Undertakers'. Addressed equally to the
imagination and understanding of children and
adults, these tales are among the finest work of
a master storyteller.

The Goalkeeper's Revenge – Bill Naughton

**'It was the custom for lads to gather at
the street corner on summer evenings and
discuss trolleying. Spit Nolan was the
champion trolley-rider. He had very good
balance, sharp wits and he was very
brave.'**

The dramatic story of Spit Nolan is one of
thirteen in this collection of funny and stirring
tales set in the 1930s. With warmth and vigour,
Bill Naughton describes the good-humoured
exploits of a lively group of boys.

Entertaining reading from the author of *My Pal
Spadger*.

The Suitcase Kid – Jacqueline Wilson

**When my parents split up they didn't know
what to do with me ...**

My family always lived at Mulberry Cottage.
Mum, Dad, me — and Radish, my Sylvanian
rabbit. But now Mum lives with Bill the Baboon
and his three kids. Dad lives with Carrie and her
twins. And where do *I* live? I live out of a
suitcase. One week with Mum's new family, one
week with Dad's.

It's as easy as A B C. That's what everyone
says. But all I want is to go home — back to
Mulberry Cottage ...

Meet ten-year-old Andy and share her
experiences of life after divorce in this realistic,
moving, yet often very funny tale from
Jacqueline Wilson, author of *The Story of Tracey
Beaker*.

'Honest, angry, sometimes sad and always very
readable'.
The Times Educational Supplement

War Boy – Michael Foreman

**I woke up when the bomb came through
the roof.**

Lowestoft, a quiet seaside town in Suffolk, was
in the front line during World War II. Bombing
raids, fires and trips to the air-raid shelter
became almost daily events for young Michael
Foreman, growing up in the 1940s.

But gas masks were great for rude noises,
gobstoppers were still good to suck and the Hill
Green Gang could still try to beat the Ship
Road Gang. Father Christmas would tell tales of
his days as a cabin boy on the great clippers,
the old tramp could spin a good yarn round the
camp-fire, and nothing could beat Mrs Ruthern's
rabbit pie!

'... a young boy's war-world, presented with an
immediacy that you can't resist' – *Books for Keeps*

'... vivid, humorous and touching' – *Guardian*

Recipes

Beans on toast

- Small tin of beans
- Two slices of bread
- Butter or low fat spread

_____ the beans

_____ in the
microwave or oven

_____ the bread

_____ the toast on a large plate

_____ the butter on the toast

_____ the beans for 2 minutes

_____ the beans on the toast

Banana split

- One banana
- Aerosol cream
- Chocolate sauce
- I chocolate flake

_____ the banana and split it lengthways

_____ the banana in a long dish

_____ the cream along the banana

_____ some chocolate sauce over the cream

_____ the flake into the cream

Pancakes

120 g plain _____

pinch of _____

I egg

half pint _____

tablespoon of vegetable oil

1. _____ the flour into the bowl and add the _____ and most of the _____

2. Beat with a hand whisk until smooth, adding the remaining _____ as you beat.

3. Add one teaspoonful of oil to the pan and pour in a half cup of pancake batter.

4. Cook until _____ on one side. Then turn _____ .

Concrete poems

ROLLING DOWN A HILL
Colin West

I'm rolling
rolling
rolling
down

I'm rolling
down a
hill.

I'm rolling
rolling
down

I'm rolling
down it
still.

I'm rolling
down
rolling
rolling
I'm rolling

I'm rolling
down a
hill.

I'm rolling
rolling
down

But now
I'm feeling
ill.

CATERPILLARS
Leigh Woods

curly wurly crunching munching crinkling wrinkling wrinkling crinkling munching crunching wurly curly caterpillars

SUPERSTINK
Robert Froman

Big bus at the bus stop.

Ready to go again.

Big noise.

Big cloud of

retch

wheeze

gulp

choke

shudder

stifle

poison

cataarrhh

gasp

cough

ghughughughu

sneeze

aaargh

stench

katchooo

#@?!&%¢

strange

choke

snuffle

sniffle

Humorous poems

Hickory, dickory dock
Two mice ran up the clock;
The clock struck one –
But the other one got away.

Old Mother Hubbard
Went to the cupboard
To get her poor dog a bone.
When she got there,
The cupboard was bare,
And she said: OICURMT!

Humpty Dumpty sat on a wall,
Humpty Dumpty had a great fall.
All the king's horses and all the king's men
Had scrambled eggs for dinner again.

You can have –
Fried fresh fish,
Fish fried fresh
Fresh fried fish,
Fresh fish fried,
Or fish fresh fried.

A significant poet: Hilaire Belloc

Rebecca
(Who Slammed Doors for Fun and Perished Miserably)

A Trick that everyone abhors
In Little Girls is slamming Doors.
A Wealthy Banker's Little Daughter
Who lived in Palace Green, Bayswater
(By name Rebecca Offendort),
Was given to this Furious Sport.

She would deliberately go
And Slam the door like Billy-Ho!
To make her Uncle Jacob start.
She was not really bad at heart,
But only rather rude and wild;
She was an aggravating child.

It happened that a Marble Bust
Of Abraham was standing just
Above the Door this little Lamb
Had carefully prepared to Slam,
And Down it came! It knocked her flat!
It laid her out! She looked like that!

* * * * * * * *

Her Funeral Sermon (which was long
And followed by a Sacred Song)
Mentioned her Virtues, it is true,
But dwelt upon her Vices, too,
And showed the Dreadful End of One
Who goes and slams the Door for Fun.

A significant poet: Hilaire Belloc

Jack and His Pony, Tom

Jack had a little pony – Tom;
He frequently would take it from
The stable where it used to stand
And give it sugar with his hand.

He also gave it oats and hay
And carrots twenty times a day
And grass in basketfuls, and greens,
And swedes and mangolds, also beans,
And patent foods from various sources
And bread (which isn't good for horses)
And chocolate and apple-rings
And lots and lots of other things
The most of which do not agree
With Polo Ponies such as he.
And all in such a quantity
As ruined his digestion wholly
And turned him from a Ponopoly
– I mean a Polo Pony – into
A case that clearly must be seen to.
Because he swelled and swelled and swelled.
Which, when the kindly boy beheld,
He gave him medicine by the pail
And malted milk, and nutmeg ale,
And yet it only swelled the more
Until its stomach touched the floor.
And when it heaved and groaned as well
And staggered, till at last it fell
And found it could not rise again.
Jack wept and prayed – but all in vain.
The pony died, and as it died
Kicked him severely in his side.

Moral
Kindness to animals should be
Attuned to their brutality.

A significant poet: James Reeves

Spells

I dance and dance without any feet —
This is the spell of the ripening wheat.

With never a tongue I've a tale to tell —
This is the meadow-grasses' spell.

I give you health without any fee —
This is the spell of the apple-tree.

I rhyme and riddle without any book —
This is the spell of the bubbling brook.

Without any legs I run for ever —
This is the spell of the mighty river.

I fall for ever and not at all —
This is the spell of the waterfall.

Without a voice I roar aloud —
This is the spell of the thunder-cloud.

No button or seam has my white coat —
This is the spell of the leaping goat.

I can cheat strangers with never a word —
This is the spell of the cuckoo-bird.

We have tongues in plenty but speak no
names —
This is the spell of the fiery flames.

The creaking door has a spell to riddle —
I play a tune without any fiddle.

The Intruder

Two-boots in the forest walks,
Pushing through the bracken stalks.

Vanishing like a puff of smoke,
Nimbletails flies up the oak.

Longears helter-skelter shoots
Into his house among the roots.

At work upon the highest bark,
Tapperbill knocks off to hark.

Painted-wings through sun and shade
Flounces off along the glade.

Not a creature lingers by,
When clumping Two-boots comes to pry.

Sentences

The green dragon snorted in the cave.

The small alien hid under the teacher's desk.

A pond skater moves quickly over the surface of the water.

The missing watch was found on top of the bookshelf.

The sinister character hid himself near the dimly lit hotel entrance.

The beautiful actress stepped over the fallen child in her hurry to get the last taxi.

Young water spiders live for some time in the nest.

Preparing for your hamster

A hamster's cage must be 55 cm wide and 21 cm in height. It should be made of plastic or wire mesh. The top must be made with air holes for the hamster to breathe. It must have a covering on the floor of its cage. Sawdust, peat, wood shavings or cat litter can be used.

Hamsters also need straw or hay for their nests, a branch to chew or climb and a wheel fixed to the side of the cage for exercise.

A literal and figurative poem

Nettles

My son aged three fell in the nettle bed.
'Bed' seemed a curious name for those green spears,
That regiment of spite behind the shed:
It was no place for rest. With sobs and tears
The boy came seeking comfort and I saw
White blisters beaded on his tender skin.
We soothed him till his pain was not so raw.
At last he offered us a watery grin,
And then I took my hook and honed the blade
And went outside and slashed in fury with it
Till not a nettle in that fierce parade
Stood upright anymore. Next task: I lit
A funeral pyre to burn the fallen dead.
But in two weeks the busy sun and rain
Had called up tall recruits behind the shed:
My son would often feel sharp wounds again.

Vernon Scannell

Written and oral storytelling

Reading the opening of Cinderella	Telling the opening of Cinderella	Notes from written story	Key to feelings
There was once a girl whose mother had died. When her father remarried, his new wife brought the two daughters from her first marriage to the house. These daughters took an instant dislike to their new sister. They threw everything out of her room into the attic. Instead of treating her like a sister, they made her do all the work. Even when she finished her jobs, she wasn't allowed to join the rest of the family. Instead she had to spend her time by the dying kitchen fire, warming her hands above the cinders – which is how she came to be called Cinderella.	Cinderella never forgot the day her two stepsisters arrived. *(long pause)* They **burst** in, <u>asked</u> where her room was, <u>told</u> her she couldn't stay in that room any longer – and threw everything out and into the attic. *(emphasise these words)* Then they told her she was to be their new servant – and live in the kitchen. They found her once, *(act out Cinderella warming her hands)* warming her hands over the cinders; and made fun of her: **'Cinders, Cinders, dirty little Cinders!'** *(use a teasing, nasty voice)*	Stepsisters arrive

Move her to attic

Does all the work – cold in kitchen – cinders – Cinderella | Hate new sister

Jealous

Very sad
Sisters becoming more spiteful |

Notes for remaining events:

Sisters receive invitation to Ball.   They make themselves beautiful.   Cinderella cries in kitchen.

Fairy Godmother arrives.   Coach, horses, footmen, drivers are made.   Beautiful dress.

Prince falls in love with her.   Midnight – slipper left!   Cinderella tries it on.

Marriage.

Guidelines for a storyteller

1. Read a myth, legend or fable you enjoy, several times.

2. Write the key events of the story as notes on cards or on a strip of paper. Identify with how the characters feel.

3. Practise telling the story, referring to your notes. Keep to the order of events and think about the effect you will have on your audience. **You do not have to use the exact words of the story as it is written down – you can shorten or lengthen sections for effect.**

4. Think about how to use your voice, body and face for effect and **when** you will:
   - speak loudly
   - speak quietly
   - speak slowly
   - speak quickly
   - pause for effect
   - stand up
   - point
   - look into the distance
   - use gestures and face to convey emotions – anger, despair, happiness, anxiety

5. Practise telling the story around the group.

6. Practise the story again, trying not to look at your notes.

7. Begin – **BUT NOT UNTIL EVERYONE HAS THEIR EYES ON YOU. WAIT UNTIL THEY'RE READY!** Your aim is to tell this story so that everyone is listening and interested.

8. Remember to look around the group. Catch the eyes of the audience.

9. Your aim is that the audience are inside the story, living it, being there!

Explanations

Fossil fuels

Fossil fuels are materials which are found naturally within the Earth's crust and are used as a source of energy.

Examples of these are coal, oil and natural gas.

These are all used as sources of energy for heating homes, powering machinery to produce factory goods and running cars for both business and pleasure.

Coal and oil are being used up rapidly and natural gas is diminishing.

As these materials diminish, new sources of energy have been invented, for example LPG (liquid petroleum gas), biodiesel (produced from rapeseed oil) and hydrogen, which is found in great quantities everywhere on Earth.

Fossil fuels

Fossil fuels are materials which are found naturally within the Earth's crust and are used as a source of energy. *(Definition)*

Examples of these are coal, oil and natural gas. *(Examples or parts)*

These are all used as sources of energy for heating homes, powering machinery to produce factory goods and running cars for both business and pleasure. *(Cause and effect – or how they work)*

Coal and oil <u>are being used up</u> rapidly and natural gas <u>is diminishing</u>. *(Interesting comments)*

As these materials diminish, new sources of energy <u>have been invented</u>, for example LPG (liquid petroleum gas), biodiesel (produced from rapeseed oil) and hydrogen, which is found in great qualities everywhere on Earth. *(Interesting comments, special features)*

How a washing machine works

Washing machines wash clothes.

Every machine has a metal drum and a motor which makes it work.

Water goes into the machine and is heated.

The machine goes through the full cycle needed to wash the clothes properly.

The machine rinses the clothes several times, with clean water.

Some washing machines also dry the clothes.

My Mum washes the clothes at night because it is cheaper.

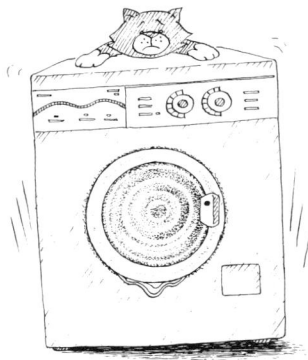

Washing machines wash clothes. **Definition**

Every machine has a metal drum and a motor which makes it work. **Parts – cause and effect**

Water goes into the machine and it is heated. **How it works**

The machine goes through the full cycle needed to wash the clothes properly. **How it works**

The machine rinses the clothes several times, with clean water. **How it works**

Some washing machines also dry the clothes. **Special features**

My Mum washes the clothes at night because it is cheaper. **Interesting comment**

Writing sentences

Adding conjunctions

- The weather was cold. She wore her boots.
- Toast the bread. Do not let it burn.
- I was five. My mother left home.
- He turned away. The flames grew bigger.
- We were hungry. We hadn't eaten all day. Our tummies were rumbling.
- The wind blew. The leaves swirled down. The team played on.

Deletion or substitution?

- The fly was buzzing in the hot room which was grimy and smelled a bit.
- Grandad used to sit on the park bench which was old and battered but he didn't notice it because it was the nearest one to the gate.
- As the wind blew the trees sent a shower of raindrops down to the earth.
- The alien daydreamed throughout the warm and sunny and hot day. He was dreaming of his blue planet he had left behind and of the yellow trees singing their songs.

Using commas to help the reader understand

- After tea, Grandfather arrived.
- Phoebe helped her mother, who was a good cook, make the cake.
- He was crying, so his mother tried to calm him down.
- He went home in a bad temper, feeling unhappy.
- Further round the left-hand side of the wall, you see an iron door, and a shadow falling upon it.
- A small, stocky, fair-haired man in a beaded coat stands facing you, a dagger in his hand.
- Where water lies underground, wells are dug to pump the water to the surface.

Musical clauses

Subject	Something about him/her/it – appearance, feelings	What he/she/it did
Harry,	small and skinny for his age,	cooked the bacon for breakfast.
James,		
Cinderella,		
Babe,		
Captain Hook,		
Superman,		
Tom,		
The Lion King,		

Old and new versions of *Snow White*

	Snow White	Snow White in New York
Characters	Snow White, King, New Queen, Huntsman, 7 dwarfs, Prince	
Setting	Palace, Forest	
Storyline	• Mother dies, father re-marries. • New Queen is jealous at Snow White's beauty. • Arranges to have her killed. • This fails: Snow White lost in the wood. • Befriended by 7 dwarfs. • Step-mother tries 3 times to kill her. • Poisoned apple lodges in throat. • Snow White unconscious, placed in coffin. • Prince falls in love, has coffin carried to palace. • Apple dislodges, Snow White comes to life. • Marries Prince.	

Film and book version of *Goodnight Mr Tom*

Film version	Book version
Radio broadcast of war against Germany.	
Mr Oakley seen in the church.	
He is heard talking in a gruff manner.	
He is seen from a distance looking at a gravestone, with a woman looking sympathetically at him.	
Refugees seen on train; Willie looking pensive.	
Train arrives: refugees seen on the station as a forlorn group.	
Mr Tom watches refugees being dropped off at different houses.	
Billetting officer brings Willie to the door.	
She states that Willie is to stay there and why and walks off briskly into the distance.	
Mr Tom asks Willie inside.	
(Snatches of sad music throughout the piece; village setting)	

Version I prefer, and why . . .

A closer look at characters

Title of book :_____

Author: _____

Type of story: _____

Narrator: name of character who tells the story. Good or bad character?	Her/his feelings.
A second character's name. Good or bad character?	Why they are in the book – how the author uses them as part of the story.
A third character's name. Good or bad character?	Why they are in the book – how the author uses them as part of the story.
A fourth character's name. Good or bad character?	Why they are in the book – how the author uses them as part of the story.
A minor character. Good or bad character?	Why they are in the book – how the author uses them as part of the story.
A minor character. Good or bad character?	Why they are in the book – how the author uses them as part of the story.

Jack and the Beanstalk as it's never been told

Jack's story – my visit to the giant's castle at the top of the beanstalk

The Giant's story – the day I was robbed!

Jack's mother's story – my life after Jack went up the beanstalk

Myths, legends and fables

Name of story:

Myth	Y	N	Legend	Y	N	Fable	Y	N
Has a god?			The main character really lived on Earth?			Animals can speak?		
Has a goddess?			The story is based on a real event?			Is a very short story?		
Has a hero who is good/bad/vain?			Places or things mentioned in the story can be traced?			Action happens and develops quickly?		
Magical things happen?			It happened a long time ago?			One character behaves badly/unwisely/stupidly?		
Characters can do fantastic things?			Things may have been added to the story over time?			A moral is at the end of the story?		

Myth – an ancient story of gods or heroes which addresses a problem or concern which humans experience *e.g. jealousy, love, hatred.*

Legend – a traditional story about heroes such as King Arthur, which may be based on truth, but which has 'grown' over the years.

Fable – a short story written to teach a moral lesson.

Narcissus: ancient and modern

Setting: Ancient Greece	Setting:
Name: Narcissus Sex: male	Name: _____ a pop music/film star Sex: male/female
Appearance: tall, blonde, blue eyes	Appearance:
Style of clothes: tunic and sandals	Style of clothes:
Theme: vanity	Theme: vanity
He admires himself in the mirror and gets dressed – Greek style	He/she admires himself/herself in the mirror and gets dressed – modern style
Echo tries to talk to him but fails	A fan called _____ approaches him/her...but fails in efforts to declare love.
He falls in love with his own reflection in a pool of water	He/she falls in love with his/her own reflection in luxury swimming pool
His parents try to make him leave	His/her manager tries to make him/her leave
He kills himself with a knife	He/she kills himself/herself by............

New facts about sparrows

Write a report on sparrows using these facts.

What do they eat?
Almost anything:
- insects and seeds
- scraps of food
- bread

Where do they live?
- towns
- villages
- farms

Breeding?
3–6 eggs hatch after 12–14 days

Appearance?
- grey and brown
- 15 cm in length

Other information?
- the number of sparrows has dropped recently
- noisy birds

A critic for a day – visual images

Title of book: _____

Author: _____

Page numbers _____ to _____.

Photograph		Picture	
Subject matter obvious?		Subject matter obvious?	
Sharp image?		Colours and style are suitable?	
Does it catch the eye?		Does it catch the eye?	
Does it help explain the text?		Does it help explain the text?	

Text which goes with the photo/picture: _____

_____

_____

_____

_____

_____

Does it help to explain the picture? _____

_____

_____

_____

Rating out of 5 ☐

A critic for a day – reference book

Feature	Yes	No	Rating (out of 5)
cover			
synopsis			
contents			
introduction			
chapter headings			
sub headings			
layout			
different types of font			
mix of photos, pictures, diagrams, charts			
index			
other features			

Would you improve on anything?

_____

Rating for the above features:

_____

Rating for the photos/pictures and quality of text:

_____

Total:

_____

Spinning their magic

After reading and discussing the poem with a friend, colour in the statements you agree with. Remember that anything you colour in you may have to talk about!

I liked the story.

The characters(s) were interesting.

After I had read it I wanted to read some more by the same poet.

I was a bit scared but I liked it.

I loved the way the poet used words.

I could see the characters as I was reading.

I knew how the characters felt.

I wanted to read on to the end.

It made me laugh.

I liked the way the poet built up the tension.

I could see the places as I was reading.

I wanted to be in that poem while things were happening.

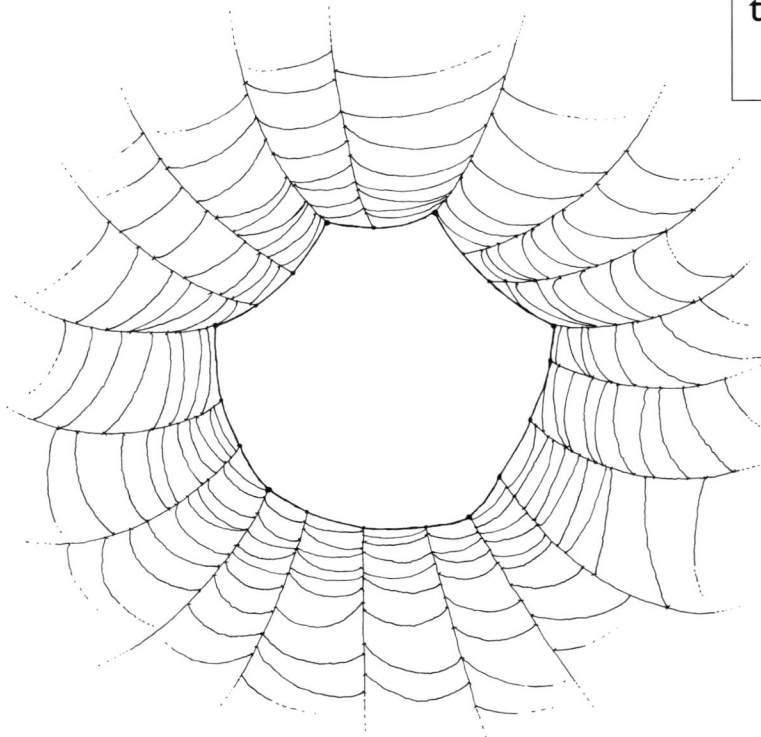

A narrative poem

The Way Through the Woods

They shut the road through the woods
Seventy years ago.
Weather and rain have undone it again,
And now you would never know
There was once a road through the woods
Before they planted the trees.
It is underneath the coppice and heath,
And the thin anemones.
Only the keeper sees
That, where the ring-dove broods,
And the badgers roll at ease,
There was once a road through the woods.

Yet, if you enter the woods
Of a summer evening late,
When the night-air cools on the trout-ringed pools
Where the otter whistles his mate
(They fear not men in the woods,
Because they see so few),
You will hear the beat of a horse's feet,
And a swish of a skirt in the dew,
Steadily cantering through
The misty solitudes,
As though they perfectly knew
The old lost road through the woods…
But there is no road through the woods!

Rudyard Kipling

Compare and contrast

Gregory Cool on arriving in Tobago

His relationship with:
- his grandparents

- Lennox

His attitude to where he lives, what he eats and the climate:

Gregory Cool after 3 days in Tobago

His relationships with:
- his grandparents

- Lennox

His attitude to where he lives, what he eats and the climate:

Points of view

Title of book:
Author:
Summary of an episode or event in the book:
The viewpoint of the character telling the reader about what is happening:
The viewpoint of another character who sees/witnesses this event (write it in the first person or third person):

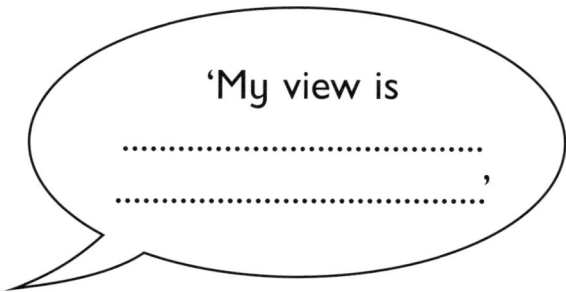

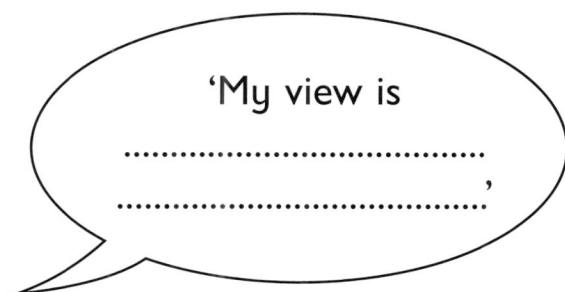

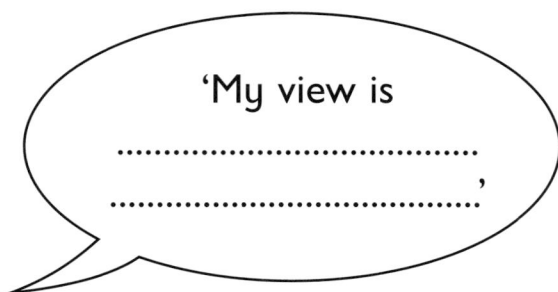

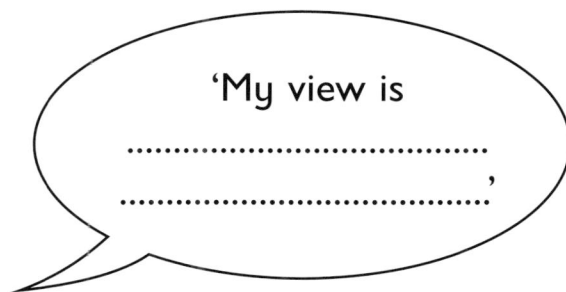

'My view is ....,'

'My view is ....,'

'My view is ....,'

'My view is ....,'

Performance poetry

Why I chose this poem.

Tick the statements below and/or make up some of your own.

I liked what it is about

I think other people would be interested

I think other people would find it funny

It has an easy rhyme pattern

The poet is speaking directly to the readers

It repeats things

It asks questions

It ....

It ....

It ....

How I will perform it

Advice on how to perform	Lines/words from the poem
I will say these lines/words quietly	
I will say these lines/words loudly	
I will say these lines/words quickly	
I will say these lines/words slowly	
I will pause here	
I will look around at my audience	
I will use gestures	
I will	

Performance poem

The Weather

What's the weather on about?
Why is the rain so down on us?
Why does the sun glare at us so?

Why does the hail dance so prettily?
Why is the snow such an overall?
Why is the wind such a tearaway?

Why is the mud so fond of our feet?
Why is the ice so keen to upset us?
Who does the weather think it is?

Gavin Ewart

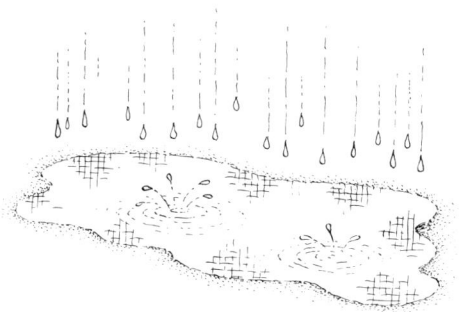

Letters

A – to inform

Dear Residents,

I am writing to inform you that the unfenced stream running alongside your properties has now been fenced in.

This was brought about because of the incident six weeks ago when a parent walking her children home from school slipped on the path and nearly fell into the stream.

We were alerted to this and used our emergency funds to sort out this problem.

I hope that this remedy is to your satisfaction.
Yours sincerely

M.K. Richards (Chairman of the Local Council)

Letters

B – to protest

Dear Sir,

We recently read about plans to close the local cinema in the village.

We are very angry about this as a promise was made only two months ago to keep the cinema open.

We have an increasingly elderly population in the village who cannot afford to use their cars to drive into the nearest town.

Also, the youngsters in the village love the Saturday morning shows.

This decision really must be discussed with the whole village.

A petition with 300 signatures has been sent with this letter.

Shame on you.

Mrs E. Major

Letters

C – to complain

Dear Headteacher,

I am writing to complain about the behaviour of some of your pupils when boarding the local bus.

For three days in a row I have needed to catch the 3.40pm bus from outside your school.

Every single day I have been pushed to one side as a certain group of children from your school boarded the bus.

I asked the driver to speak to them but he said it was nothing to do with him. He suggested I write a letter of complaint to you.

I am very annoyed about this – when I was young we always showed respect to our elders, but it seems that this is no longer the case!

From a very angry OAP.

Yours sincerely

Mr J.B. Williams

Letters

D – to persuade

Dear Parent,

I am writing to tell you about our new strawberry toothpaste, which has just been launched in your area.

This product took three years to research and has been proven to prevent tooth decay more effectively than any other product on the market.

Children love the taste and choose this flavour more than any other on the market!

What is good taste makes good sense!

At the bottom of the letter you will find a free voucher for 3 tubes of our new product. At no cost to you, this product can be tried out: we hope you will agree that this is without a doubt the most effective toothpaste ever created.

Hope you like the product!

P.C. Masters (Managing Director)

Features cards

A – to inform
√ Formal opening sentence gives key piece of information
√ Several examples of why the writer is doing this
√ A concluding statement
√ A formal ending

B – to protest
√ Opening statement states what the protest is about
√ Following sentences offer reasons in support of the protest – e.g. why things should not change
√ Angry, emotional tone and phrases, including the letter ending (alternatively this could be formal but assertive)

C – to complain
√ Opening sentence states what the complaint is
√ Following sentences give further reasons to back up the complaint
√ Angry, emotional tone and phrases, including the letter ending (Alternatively the tone might be formal but assertive)

D – to persuade
√ Opening sentence states what the writer wants you to know about
√ Following sentences offer evidence/reasons which are aimed to persuade you to think or do something
√ Pleasant, upbeat tone
√ Casual, friendly ending

Advertisements

Advertisement or flier for: _____

Feature	Who is it written for?				
Rating out of 5	1	2	3	4	5
Layout – what do you look at first and why?					
Information – what is the big message?					
Language – what types of words and phrases have been chosen? What tense is used?					
Opinion – is a view or opinion given as if it is a fact?					
Illustrations – are they effective?					
Colour and font – do the choices support the type of text?					
Is there anything you would change? Why?					

Car advertising

A)

> If you fancy a refreshing change, check out the new ....
>
> Only .... on the road.
>
> The new .... includes:
> * Power steering
> * Driver's airbag
> * CD player
> * Immobilizer

B)

> The .... has a beautifully balanced chassis, precision-weighted controls and deft steering.

C)

> INTRODUCING THE NEW ....
> A DIFFERENT KIND OF FAMILY CAR.
> The new............................. boasts a 250 bhp 5 cylinder turbine engine.
> Plus........................

D)

> Have you noticed how hard it is to
> be individual these days? And have
> you ever wondered why?
> To be different, the true individual
> you know you are, be seen in the
> new ....

E)

> Ready, steady, go. You will in the new .... It packs power steering, central locking, driver's airbag, leather steering wheel, a punchy 1.3 engine and blue-trimmed interior. All for........................

F)

> But the ....isn't just about extremely good value and style. It's also about safety, with twin airbags and side impact protectors.

G)

> .... The right car.
> .... The secret of success.

Points of view

Description of material (film, song, article, report, photograph, poem etc.)	Point of view being expressed
Folk song – *If I Had A Hammer*	Humans living in peace and harmony
Whalesong – poem	
Article on pollution	

Argument frame

Name: _____

Date: _____

We believe that _____

_____

_____

There are several reasons which support our view.
To begin with there is evidence that _____

_____

_____

Furthermore, we know that _____

_____

_____

Moreover, it has been proved that _____

_____

_____

Therefore, although some people think that _____

_____

_____

We think that we have shown, without any doubt, that _____

_____

_____

Spelling and definitions

Word	Correctly spelled?	Correct spelling	Definition
insinerate			
radiant			
silhouette			
turpentyne			
evaperate			
compliment			
incessant			
scenick			
steeplejack			
wrestle			

Slang

swell

fusty

mint

soppy

frowsy

ace

brill

lush

fab

gross

ripping

cool

groovy

chronic

neat

bad

mega

wicked

rotten

radical

spiffing

Benny McEever

Benny McEever
Two left feet
Lived in a council house
On Poverty Street.
Never knew his mother
His dad was on the rocks
Lived down the Embankment
In a cardboard box.
His gran once told him
She'd seen him around
Playing a cornet for pennies
Down the Underground.
Benny McEever
Holes in his shoes
Never lost nothing
Nothing to lose.
'Cept a mouthpiece off a cornet
Had once been his dad's
That his grandmother found
one day
And gave to the lad.
And Benny learned to play it
Played mournful and sad
Melodies about the love
Poor Benny never had.
Dirty-neck Benny
Brillo-pad hair
Wore a sign on his face
Said, 'I don't care.'
Benny had a heart
Like a dried-up well
Love was a word
He never learned to spell.
His school said Benny
Was a real dead loss
His brain was stuffed
With candy floss.

Kids moved aside
To let him pass
He sat on his own
At the back of the class.

Started playing truant
Wandered all alone
Aimless and friendless
All around the town.
Walked into a jewellery shop
Saw a gold watch there
Slipped it in his pocket
Ran out into the square.
Back in the schoolyard
The whisper went round,
'Seen Benny's watch?
Cost two hundred pound!
Where d'you get it, Benny?'
They all asked jealously
And proudly Benny answered,
'My dad bought it me.'
He hadn't really meant it
The lie had been a game
But the more he repeated it
The truer it became.

When Benny ran home
His gran was outside
With two tall policemen
Standing by her side.
And Benny started running
The wind in his hair
Through back yards and
alleyways
It didn't matter where.
Fear screamed inside his skull
He felt his wild heart beat
And always behind him
The sound of running feet.

Benny McEever

He dashed through the market
Dodging in and out
And the air was filled with
whistling
Sirens and shouts.
At last behind the roller rink
He fell to the floor
Poor Benny McEever
Couldn't run anymore.

In front of the magistrate
Hangdog Billy stood.
The social worker told the court,
'It must be in his blood.
His mother wasn't any good
His father was the same.
If you ask me, Your Honour,
Heredity's to blame.'

'I just can't control him,'
His grandmother said.
'Won't do anything I say
Just lies all day in bed.'

Benny in a special school
Lost and alone
Felt his heart turning
Into a stone.
He took out the mouthpiece
That he kept on a string
Pressed it softly to his lips
And made the metal sing.
It sang a song of heartbreak
That made the sad stars weep
Till finally, still playing,
Benny fell asleep.
Then one day Benny
Went walking by the shore

Past cranes and ships and
dockyards
Where he'd never walked before.
Heard footsteps close behind him
Strange voices everywhere
But when Benny turned to look
around
Nobody was there.
Benny stood frozen
Heard the seagull's cries
While the sea mist descended
Like a scarf about his eyes.
Benny running blindly
Down Dead End Lane
Heard a voice whispering
Benny's own name.
'Benny McEever
There's nothing to fear
Come on up, Benny,
I'm waiting for you here.'

Better run, Benny,
You'd better beware
But everywhere that Benny ran
The voice was always there.
Found his feet walking
Up stairs, across a floor
Found his hand turning
The handle of a door.
And the voice spoke softly
Cutting Benny like a knife,
'I've been waiting for you, Benny,
The whole of our life.'
Benny saw a figure
Sitting all alone
Face as old as Charity
Eyes like a stone.

Benny McEever

His boots let water
His coat was a sack
His hands were bent and buckled
His fingernails black.
He called Benny over
The soft voice was sad.
He said,
'I want to tell you, Benny
All about your dad.
I knew him well, Benny.'
And the old man's eyes
were calm.
'I was closer to your father
Than my own right arm.
It was only bad luck
That led him astray
He was never as bad
As people might say.'
Then he took out a bundle
And said with a sigh,
'Your dad sent you this
To remember him by.'
Benny's nervous fingers
Untied the string.
He found a battered trumpet
Lying there within.
He stuck on the mouthpiece
Blew strong and bold
And the sweet notes cascaded

Like a shower of gold.
'Tell my dad...' said Benny
But nobody was there
Just a door swinging slowly,
The room quite bare.

And Benny strode out
Past the cranes and the ships
His dad's battered cornet
Pressed to his lips.
And a host of children
Skipped after the boy
Their voices raised high
In an anthem of joy.
And the song they sang
Soared sweet and high
Blowing like a tempest
Across the sky.
It screamed through the
schoolroom
It roared through the port
It scattered the papers
In the magistrate's court.
And Benny remembered
His whole life long
How one great Good
Could drive out every Wrong.

Gareth Owen

Classic books

Ballet Shoes

The Water Babies

Charlotte's Web

Winnie the Pooh

The Box of Delights

The Eagle of the Ninth

The Borrowers

Mary Poppins

The Hobbit

The Secret Garden

Just William

Great Expectations

Alice in Wonderland

Robinson Crusoe

The Wizard of Oz

Peter Pan

Little House in the Big Woods

The Children of Green Knowe

A Little Princess

The Voyage of the Dawn Treader

Treasure Island

The Railway Children

Little Women

Gulliver's Travels

The Wind in the Willows

Just So Stories

The Coral Island

The Lion, the Witch and the Wardrobe

Book review

Title:

Author:

First published:

Something about the author:

What it is all about (problem, developments, characters, setting):

What I got from the story (what I learnt, my feelings about the characters, what I thought about the writer's style...):

Why someone else should read it:

Star Rating: ☆ ☆ ☆ ☆ ☆

Sentences

Finding the main clause

1. The greyish-green grasshopper chirped in the long grass at the bottom of our garden.

2. The yacht with the red sails bobbed merrily on the glistening blue sea.

3. She was playing her trumpet at the concert for elderly people in the village.

4. Kathryn was sipping her cool wine in the shade of the rose tree.

5. Every Saturday Grandad liked strolling aimlessly in the park far from his tiny, cramped flat.

Sentence beginnings

They found oil	Jamie missed the tram	She took off her slippers	He left the concert
There were six of them in the river	The stage fell down	The doctor did not come	She ran and ran
The woman did not move	No award will be made	It was a lovely day	The dress was cheap

Joining three sentences

Join three sentences then write a mini-story of no more than 50 words.

Select from the following conjunctions:
so, because, if, but, before, although

You have difficulty in hearing. I will not sell you this DVD player. It is unsuitable.

I do not know. I saved the alien's letter. I received it last Friday.

The explorer found the entrance to the cavern. He saw the gaping hole. He could not stop himself falling.

You are poor. I think you must work even harder for me. I know you hate me.

The forger made thousands of notes. He knew they might be spotted. He did not care.

Reports

The literacy work this week has been concerned with reports of events. These are called recounts.

Children have studied recounts and learned about the features of a recount and how to write one of their own.

The sentence level focus has been about the need for standard English when writing for an unknown audience such as a newspaper reader; they have also looked at the differences between direct and indirect speech.

With your child, find a recount of a sporting event and another recount of something which has happened. See if you can fill in all the boxes for the 5 'W's – these should be present in reports like these.

Headline	
Who	
What	
When	
Why	
Where	
Headline	
Who	
What	
When	
Why	
Where	

Playscripts

The literacy work this week has been concerned with playscripts.

Children have read a playscript and thought carefully about how to perform it as the author would have wished it.

They have studied playscripts carefully and written one of their own, based on extracts from Roald Dahl books.

They have proof-read and edited these scripts and put them into a class Big Book.

Turn this extract from a story into a playscript.

She walked slowly through the forest, enjoying the warmth of the sun on her bare arms. David, her brother, had walked on ahead and she could no longer see him in the gloom of the pine forest looming ahead. She moved into the cool area of the forest, her footsteps sinking into the springy green moss.

'David, David,' she called. 'Where are you? Stop hiding!'
'I'm here, Kay,' he whispered.
'Where? I can't see you!'
Then she noticed the arm around his neck. . .

'Stop fooling around, Davey – Grandpa's behind me with Beth the Alsatian – he'll send her after you if you don't come out! Grandpa, grandpa. . .'

The first thing she heard was a bump as David was pushed to the ground, then she saw a dark shadow fleeing away. . .
'You saved my life, Kay,' gasped David, picking himself off the forest floor.

Note-making

> The literacy work this week has been concerned with how to make notes from information books.
> Children have read a selection of texts and learned how to make notes which use the smallest possible number of words. The word level focus has been on the use of abbreviations as an economical way of writing while still communicating meaning.

Read the information below and make notes. You can use labelled pictures, think of headings for each section and make a bullet point list – but do not write more than 30 words. Give an adult the information to read and keep while you sum up the information using your notes alone. Ask them how well you did.

Keeping cool

Animals that live in hot deserts have found ways of surviving in the hot, dry climate. Many of them move about at night, when it is cool. During the day, they shelter under rocks and plants, or in burrows. The animals that do move around in the daytime heat often have ways of keeping their bodies away from the burning sand. The Saharan jerboa and the American kangaroo rat have long back legs to hop quickly over the ground. The frilled lizard of the Australian desert also runs on its back legs.

Creatures such as snakes and lizards, which are cold-blooded, need to warm themselves in the heat of the sun before they can move around. They hide in the shade when the sun is at its hottest.

The main problem for desert animals is the lack of water. Some have found ways of storing water in their bodies. Others get all the moisture they need from the plants and insects they eat, and hardly ever need to drink at all.

Punctuation

The literacy work this week has been concerned with story openings.

Children have read a range of openings, comparing how different stories begin in different ways.

The sentence level focus has been on proof-reading and editing skills, checking their own writing for meaning and correct spelling and punctuation (including the punctuation of dialogue).

Put in all the missing punctuation in this extract.

She walked slowly through the forest enjoying the warmth of the sun on her bare arms David her brother had walked on ahead and she could no longer see him in the gloom of the pine forest looming ahead She moved into the cool area of the forest her footsteps sinking into the springy green moss.

David David she called Where are you Stop hiding
I'm here Kay he whispered
Where I can't see you
Then she noticed the arm around his neck . . .

Then turn the text into a dialogue between you and an adult where you tell them what happened.

Characters

The literacy work this week has been concerned with how writers depict characters and make you take a positive or negative view of them.

Children have read extracts and analysed how writers do this, and have imitated the style of the writer in a short piece of dialogue.

The sentence level focus has been on proof-reading and editing skills, checking their own writing for meaning and correct spelling and punctuation, including the punctuation of dialogue.

Read a chapter of the fiction book which your child has brought home and fill in the table below, together.

Title of book	
Name of character	
Actions	
Appearance	
Feelings	
Author's intention	

Books we enjoy

The literacy work this week has been concerned with thinking about books your children have enjoyed – and getting them to explain why they liked them.

We also thought about books which have been around for some time, and just what makes these books still appeal to children today!

Finally, the children thought carefully about what writers base their books on – real or/and imagined experiences – and enjoyed listening to a book by Michael Morpurgo which was based on a mixture of both.

Books we loved as children

This is an important questionnaire linked to the work in literacy for the week.

The class would like to put together the results in a book to be displayed in school.

Children have already used a sheet like this – now it is your turn.

Please fill this in together and return it to school as soon as you can.

If you still own the book you loved, please send it to school for a display. We will look after it.

The book I really like – and why.

Title: _____

Author: _____

Date of publication: _____

When I first read this book: _____

_____

Why I first read this book: _____

_____

What I liked about it: _____

_____

Instructions

> The literacy work this week has been concerned with instructions.
> The sentence level focus has been on using the correct tense for instructions – the present tense – and using imperative verbs such as 'take', 'cut', 'stick' etc.

All the imperative verbs have been left out in this recipe.
Fill them in and then follow the instructions, adding your own topping!

Pizza Bases
1/4 pint of warm water
225 g plain or wholemeal flour
1/2 teaspoon of dried yeast
1 tablespoon of oil

Sp_____ the yeast onto the
warm water, st_____ and s_____ aside
until the mixture bubbles. St_____
in the oil, then gradually a_____
this liquid to the flour. T_____
the dough onto a floured board
and kn_____ for 5–10 minutes
to make a soft, elastic dough.
Di_____ the mixture into four,
and r_____ out to make 4 thin circles.
Pl_____ on a lightly greased baking
sheet and b_____ for 5 minutes at
200°C/400°F.
Arr_____ the topping on the bases
and c_____ for 10–15 minutes more.

Choose the words which make sense!

arrange/arrive; dish/divide; rub/roll; stamp/stir; spread/sprinkle; set/stand;
twist/turn; knot/knead; place/plan; boil/bake; cuddle/cook; add/act;

Metaphors

The literacy work this week has been concerned with poems which are fun and play around with words. Children have heard and told jokes which play on words.

They have also been listening to and trying out metaphors.

A metaphor says that *one thing is another*: it makes you think about something in a really vivid, dramatic way and is used for effect by poets and writers.

Help your child by teaching him/her some tongue twisters:

* She sells sea shells on the sea shore.
* Peter Piper picked a peck of pickled peppers.
  If Peter Piper picked a peck of pickled peppers, where's the peck of pickled peppers Peter Piper picked?'

Use a joke book to find some jokes which play on words – your child should already know some.

Help your child fill in nouns in the first set of circles and verbs, adverbs and adjectives in the outside circles.

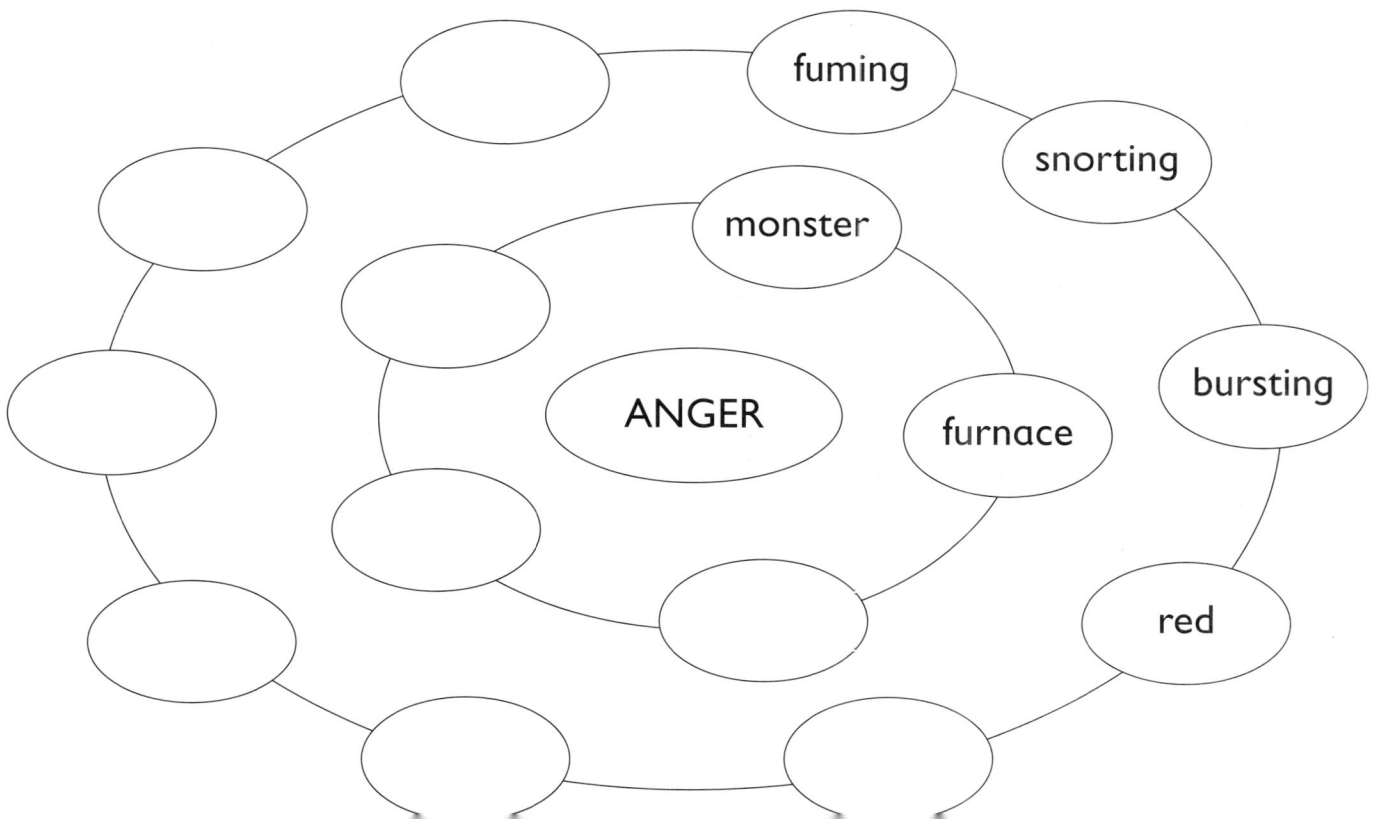

fuming

snorting

monster

bursting

ANGER

furnace

red

Poetry

The literacy work this week has been about looking closely at how poems are written and the differences between two different poets. Your children will have looked at the poetry of Hillaire Belloc and James Reeves.

Choose a poem together from the poetry book your child has brought home.

Read the poem then decide whether to tick the the 'Yes' or 'No' box.

	Yes	No
Words create pictures in my mind		
Every line rhymes		
Some words rhyme in one line		
Some lines are longer than others		
Very short lines, including one word lines		
Each verse is the same length		
Repetition of lines		
Repetition of words		
Questions		
Poem is in a particular shape		
Poem tells a story		
Poem is serious		
Poem is funny		
Poet uses similes		
Poet uses metaphors		
Dialogue appears in the poem		

Punctuation

The literacy work this week has been concerned with the structure of sentences and the use of punctuation within the sentence. Children have also studied how to write an information sheet for a younger audience.

Read and study French Fries then complete the sentences which follow.

French Fries
You will need the following ingredients: potatoes, cooking oil, salt.

Mashed Banana Sandwich

You will _____

Cheese and Pickle Sandwich

You will _____

_____

Read the sentence about dinosaurs then put in the missing commas in the three sentences which follow.

Dinosaurs, the biggest and most vicious creatures who have ever roamed Earth, disappeared from the face of this planet.

Sebastian the biggest and strongest Rottweiler dog I had ever seen bounded towards me and started licking my hand.

Michael Smith the fastest footballer in our school team chose me for Captain.

Mum tall and blonde fell in love with my dad short and dark.

Poetry

The literacy work this week has been concerned with narrative poems and raps. Children have read a range of narrative poems which tell a story, noted the story inside and then presented the poems in different ways.

There is no better way for your child to really get to know a poem than by learning it off by heart. Please read this poem with your child and help him/her to remember it

Three Fishers Went Sailing

Three fishers went sailing out into the West,
Away to the West as the sun went down;
Each thought on the woman that loved him the best,
And the children stood watching them out of the town:
For men must work, and women must weep,
And there's little to earn, and many to keep,
Though the harbour-bar be moaning.

Three wives sat up in the lighthouse tower,
And they trimmed their lamps as the sun went down;
And they looked at the squall and they looked at the shower,
And the night-rack came rolling up ragged and brown;
But men must work, and women must weep,
Though storms be sudden, and waters deep
And the harbour-bar be moaning.

Three corpses lay out on the shining sands,
In the morning gleam as the sun went down,
And the women are weeping and wringing their hands,
For those who will never come back to the town.
For men must work, and women must weep,
And the sooner it's over, the sooner to sleep,
And goodbye to the bar and its moaning.

Charles Kingsley

Storytelling

The literacy work this week has been concerned with storytelling. Children have read fairy tales, myths and legends and changed them into a spoken rather than a written form.

It would be very useful if you would tell your child a tale/story you may have been told as a child, or describe something funny that happened when your child was a baby.

Ask your child to write some notes down then practise telling your story to you.

The class teacher will hold a 'Storytelling Session' during a lunch hour next week – you are invited to come along!

My Dad's/Mum's story: my notes

Information texts

The literacy work this week has been concerned with texts which give information, in particular texts which explain how things work.

We also want pupils to notice how headlines can sometimes be read in two different ways and how some words have two different meanings.

Read these headlines with your child. Discuss the meaning(s)

1. Police shot man with knife.
2. Baby Changing Room.
3. Sheep attacks rocket!
4. Girl kissed boy with apple.
5. Dog bit man with orange.

Can you think of one more?

Write in two different meanings for these words.

Bank		
Fan		
Jam		
Club		
Lie		
Grave		
Trip		
Fine		

Sentences

The literacy work this week has been concerned with writing a variety of sentences, moving words around within sentences and deleting words or changing them within sentences; all these skills are designed to make your child a more effective writer.

Headlines need to catch the eye of the reader, giving enough information to make the reader **want** to read on.

Challenge: change these sentences into interesting headlines by deleting certain words, moving others around and making any other changes you feel are necessary. For example:

The award for Footballer of the Year was won by David Beckham.

Beckham wins Footballer of the Year Award

Now do the same for the following:

The sheep was found stranded up a tree after the floods.

_____

The weather was so bad it smashed the new glass doors of the Civic Centre.

_____

The carnival at Brixton was the best one ever.

_____

The top model was found floating in the river.

_____

The children of a local primary school won all the prizes at the local show.

_____

Stories

> The literacy work this week has been concerned with comparing different versions of the same story and the filmed version of a story.

Help your child to fill in this sheet in order to produce a modern version of *Red Riding Hood* set in London in the year 2002.

Red Riding Hood	Red Riding Hood in London
Lives in a forest with mother	Lives in a flat in London with mother
Granny ill – sent on errand	
Wanders off the path	
Is spotted by Big Bad Wolf – who runs ahead	
Big Bad Wolf ties up Granny	
He pretends to be Granny	
Red Riding Hood in danger in cottage	
Passing Woodcutter saves her by killing Wolf	

Setting	Setting
Forest and Granny's cottage	

Illustrations	Illustrations
Traditional	

Narration

The literacy work this week has been concerned with how authors write their stories by using a character called a narrator to tell the story.

We have read different stories and worked out who is telling it.

The homework activity encourages your child to think carefully about what makes adventure stories so popular – is it the characters who tell the story or the story-line?

Title of adventure book: _____

Author: _____

Name of the character who is telling the story: _____

What we know about the character (appearance, feelings, views on what is going on in the story): _____

_____

Events in the story:

1 _____
2 _____
3 _____
4 _____
5 _____
6 _____
7 _____
8 _____
9 _____

On a separate piece of paper write your views on whether it was the fast-moving, exciting story-line, or the narrator's views on what was going on that kept you reading this book.

Myths, legends and fables

The literacy work this week has been about myths, legends and fables. The class has read a selection and looked carefully at the differences between them. They have written some of their own.
They have also been careful to check their use of pronouns in their written work.

Pronoun Practice!

a) In the following sentences, which nouns do the underlined pronouns refer to?

1. Mum carried the bottle to the kitchen. At the sink <u>she</u> dropped <u>it.</u>

she = _____   it = _____

2. My dad bought some comics and <u>he</u> gave <u>them</u> to me.

he = _____ them = _____

3. When the dog saw its master <u>it</u> turned and followed <u>him.</u>

it = _____   him = _____

b) Rewrite this passage using pronouns to replace most of the names. Use a separate sheet of paper.

Olivia and Henry decided to go swimming. Olivia started up Olivia's motorbike and Henry got on the back. Although Henry was a bit scared he did not tell Olivia to slow down as Henry knew Olivia would lose Olivia's temper. Olivia not only lost her temper but Olivia also lost her licence. Henry is now the sole driver of the motorbike and Henry has a great time taking Henry's friends to the local swimming pool.

c) Choose the correct pronoun from this list: *themselves, myself, herself*

• I hurt _____ when I fell. My sister also hurt _____ when she tried to save me.

• Because it was gloomy they could not see _____ in the mirror.

Information texts

The literacy work this week has been concerned with writing short information texts.

Detective Scanner!

Skimming and scanning are reading skills which are useful when hunting for facts.

Open the information book your child has brought home at any page but don't let him/her see the page you are reading.

Skim over the page quickly to see if you can find anything which interests you.

When you find something interesting, stop and read it carefully. Write the fact which interested you in the chart.

Now give the book back to your child.
Your child should look in the index for a key word from your fact, turn to the correct page and scan for the sentence, then write in the correct page number

Book title	Interesting fact	Page number

Information texts

The literacy work this week has been concerned with comparing information books with the same themes but presented in different ways. Children have analysed them and then presented a critical view. They have also discovered that authors of information books may 'borrow' photos and text from other sources. These must be acknowledged in their books.

Your child has brought home some information books on the same theme but with different authors.

Ask your child to choose three photos/diagrams/charts and one short piece of text.

Please help your child to fill in the chart by skimming and scanning for useful text and brilliant photos!

Title of book	Theme
Photo/diagrams/chart	My reasons for selecting this
Photo/diagrams/chart	
Photo/diagrams/chart	
Text – from page	

Title of book	Theme
Photo/diagrams/chart	My reasons for selecting this
Photo/diagrams/chart	
Photo/diagrams/chart	
Text – from page	

Poetry

The literacy work this week was about making a class collection of favourite poems.

The children worked together to produce some more verses based on a poem by Rudyard Kipling: *The Way Through The Woods*.

As the class have made their collection of favourite poems, they thought it would be a good idea to make a collection of their parents' favourite poems.

Please find copies of your favourite poems or browse through some of the poetry anthologies your child has brought home.

Fill in the box below then tick the boxes which show why you like this poem. Add in some more comments about your poem if you wish. Please share your homework with your child!

Name of poet	Title of poem

I like the rhythm	The choice of words creates powerful pictures	It tells a powerful story	
It makes me laugh	I like the way it rhymes	I like the layout of the words	
It makes me think about the meaning	It's fun to read aloud	The poem taught me something	

Words

The literacy work this week has been concerned with books from other cultures and traditions.

Children have looked closely at people living and working in different cultures and at the relationships, attitudes and customs which are evident, comparing these with their own experiences, if possible.

Write your definition of the meaning of each of these words.
Using an adult dictionary, check if you are close or correct, then find out where the word came from originally. Ask an adult to help you.

Word	Meaning	Country of origin
Saga		
Yoga		
Deck		
Crayon		
Avalanche		
Shampoo		
Landscape		
Husband		

Punctuation

The literacy work this week has been concerned understanding that the author presents a 'point of view' to readers through what characters say, how they act and how the author describes them.

When the children have finished their writing they have been checking meaning, punctuation and spelling, including the use of the apostrophe to show possession.

Apostrophes can show possession:

Hagrid's coat was full of pockets.
Harry's school uniform included one plain, pointed black hat.

If the person's name ends in an s, you can either add an apostrophe and another s or just add an apostrophe:

Scabbers' fur was grey and his tail was long.

For groups of people or things which end in s just add an apostrophe:

The wizards' cloaks needed dry-cleaning.

If the group of people or things does not end in an s add an apostrophe and an s

The children's book list included Magical Theory by Adalbert Waffling.

Put in the correct apostrophes in the sentences below:

Charlotte (   ) dress was deep blue.

Asif (   ) ice-cream melted in the sun.

James (   ) friends made him laugh.

The students (   ) broomsticks were stored in the broom cupboard.

The men (   ) possessions were scattered everywhere.

Now write some examples of your own.

Idiom

The literacy work this week has been concerned with poems which can be read aloud or performed in order to catch the interest of an audience.

The children have been encouraged to use a range of different dictionaries and will use the homework sheet below as a first step into using a dictionary of idioms.

Idiom	What I think it means	Dictionary definition
To know which side your bread is buttered on		
A pretty kettle of fish		
Dressed to kill		
To pull your weight		
To blow your top		
In hot water		
To throw in the towel		
To fly off the handle		
A red herring		
Salt of the earth		

Antonyms

The literacy work this week has been concerned with reading different types of letters in newspapers and magazines.
The children were encouraged to use a range of different dictionaries and will use the homework sheet below as a first step into using a dictionary of antonyms.

Word	Antonym (opposite)	Dictionary choices
neglect	Care for, consider, respect	
meek		
light		
idle		
attractive		
fresh		
serious		
clumsy		
approve		

Synonyms

The literacy work this week has been concerned with persuasive writing in fliers and advertisements.
The children have read and discussed these, looking carefully at how they have been constructed.
They have been encouraged to use a range of different dictionaries and will use the homework sheet below as a first step into using a dictionary of synonyms.

Fill in the chart below, writing synonyms you already know in the second column. Then use a dictionary to write more synonyms in the third column.

Word	Synonyms (words which are similar in meaning)	Dictionary choices
precious	Valuable, costly, treasured	
foolish		
popular		
invent		
elegance		
plain		
trick		

Dictionaries

The literacy work this week has been concerned with how points of view are presented through a range of different texts.

The children have been encouraged to use a range of different dictionaries and will use the homework sheet below as a first step into checking the meanings of scientific terms.

Word	Meaning	Dictionary definition
Circuit		
Component		
Gravity		
Friction		
Reflection		
Vibration		
Pitch		

Dictionaries

The literacy work this week has been concerned with using different types of dictionaries. Children have learnt how to find a word quickly by knowing where in the dictionary certain letters appear and how to find out the origin of words.

The sheet below has a list of words used in America.
Help your child to write in the British word.

Please add a small illustration alongside each American word.

American English	British English
vest	
trunk	
potato chips	
yard	
purse	
center	
theater	
suspenders	
gas	
diaper	
thumbtack	
sidewalk	
cookie	
color	
trash can	

Word origins

The literacy work this week has been concerned with looking carefully at the way in which viewpoints are presented in a poem. Your child has been asked to present an argument which is sympathetic to the main character in the poem.

All the words below came from Old French – see if you can match up the French and English words.

abeie

boucle

idele

curtain

chimney

idol

cortine

truele

diamant

pearl

button

carpet

povre

carpite

cheminee

buckle

abbey

feast

acuser

gelee

oignon

feste

diamond

jelly

bouton

perle

poor

onion

accuse

trowel

Beat the Clock!
You have 5 minutes to think of 15 words ending in these suffixes:

-ward	-ship	-ment	-ist	-hood

'Classics'

The literacy work this week has been concerned with 'classic' books and poems. Children have decided what makes a book a classic; read and studied classic books, poems and written in the style of a classic author. They have also decided upon a new 'Modern Classics' list.

Study the list below and discuss why these books are so popular.
A space has been left blank for you to fill in the name of a book you would like to be included on the list.
Fill in the commentary at the bottom.

Fantastic Mr Fox	Stig of the Dump	The Suitcase Kid	The Eighteenth Emergency
James and the Giant Peach	The Midnight Fox	Bill's New Frock	Why the Whales Came
The Silver Sword	Truckers	Flat Stanley	Harry Potter and the Philosopher's Stone
Goodnight Mr Tom	The Iron Man	The Sheep Pig	

Why my choice of book should be considered a 'classic':

Non-standard English

> The literacy work this week has been concerned with how different sentences are written, and how to improve them.
> The children have written a short story of no more than 50 words in standard English so that everyone could understand the meaning quite clearly.

When people are with their friends, they may use non-standard English when chatting together. This is English which is spoken, rather than written.

Change the following polite English remarks into non-standard 'chat' between friends:

'Hello, how are you?' _____

'Would you like to play football in the park with our friends?' _____

_____

'What was the result of the game on television last night?' _____

_____

Cockney Rhyming Slang
Cockney people invented this language, and it is still being used.

Barnet Fair = hair

Bacon and eggs = legs

What do you think these mean? They are all parts of the body.

Hampstead Heath = _____

Chalk Farm = _____

Boat race = _____

North and South = _____

Plates of meat = _____

Loaf of bread = _____

Mince pies = _____

What do you think this sentence means?

My wife was on the dog and bone to her skin and blister.

_____

Notes

Notes